Endorsements

I often hear quoted, "Jesus is my Redeemer" and references to His redemption are frequent in the Christian community. Seldom however, do I hear believers embrace the fact that Jesus redeems time. I love this topic and I encourage you to explore it by reading Troy Brewer's book, *Redeeming Your Timeline*—it is full of delightful revelatory insights for you.

PATRICIA KING
Minister, Author, Television Host
PatriciaKing.com

Troy Brewer has created a timeless masterpiece on the power of redemption—a supernatural life-altering book on Biblical time travel. *Redeeming Your Timeline* is guaranteed to change the way you think and more importantly the way you live. Time doesn't own you, Jesus does! Time is a gift from God and this book is a gift to the body of Christ. I am privileged to call Troy my friend and count it a joy to co-labor with him for the Kingdom. Read this book with great anticipation and see what the Lord will do for and through you, as He moves in and out of time on your behalf.

WARD SIMPSON
President, GOD TV

Troy is a brilliant fellow, but his new book *Redeeming Your Timeline* goes beyond intelligence. It is revelational. Our society is going through what I would consider a poverty mindset toward time. We do not understand the redemption available to this existence and that our God, who lives outside of time and space, wants to bring it to us. When we understand that time is one of our most important resources (like food, sleep, water) then we will steward it as a treasured priority. Not only that, we will understand the nature of God and how He brings Himself into our timeline again and again out of His great love for us. This is such a good read—full of new ideas as well as redefining old ones—you need to read it and get a good dose of *spiritual intelligence* concerning God redeeming your timeline.

SHAWN BOLZ
Author of *Translating God, Keys To Heaven's Economy,* and *Through the Eyes of Love*
TV Host on TBN
Podcast host of the Exploring Series on Charisma Podcast Network

Troy Brewer's revelation of how God can bring redemption into your life—dealing with your pains, hurts and defeats, without respect to time—can set you free. Time is something that limits us, but not God. Jesus stepped out of eternity and into time, *"at just the right 'time'"* (Romans 5:6 NIV), to secure our redemption. God, not being subject to time, can step into the moments in your life that brought the most shame and humiliation and bring redemption. He can touch your timeline! Your faith will be stronger after reading this book and your love for the Lord will be more beautiful than ever before. Enjoy and be blessed.

RON CANTOR
Israel Regional Director, GOD TV
CEO Tikkun International

Troy Brewer communicates like a master storyteller making timeless truths and deep revelation both simple and accessible. This book represents the unique season we are living in as it unfolds the unprecedented exploration of the depths of redemption that occurred through the cross of our Lord Jesus Christ. *Redeeming Your Timeline* offers hope in rewriting your personal story until it matches the full measure of God's goodness.

DAN MCCOLLAM
Co-founder of Bethel School of the Prophets, The Prophetic Company, Sounds of the Nations, and author *Bending Time, God Vibrations,* and *Love and Prophecy*

In an age where time seems to be passing with increasing acceleration, never has it been more important to be intentional, missional, and fruitful with the time we have been given. This book inspires, equips, and challenges you to do exactly that, while at the same time leaning heavily on and walking hand in hand with the God who is outside of time, is present in your past, present, and future, and is able to redeem and restore all things, making something beautiful out of your whole life, for His glory. *Redeeming Your Timeline* will inspire you, challenge you, make you laugh and cry and say "wow!" over and over again! It is our great honor to highly recommend to you both this book and its brilliant author, our friend Pastor Troy Brewer. You're going to love it!

BEN & JODIE HUGHES
Pour It Out Ministries
www.pouritout.org
Authors of *When God Breaks In* and *The King's Decree*

I have spent many hours picking Troy's brain on this subject and I feel like I have only scratched the surface of what he is able to impart! The Holy Spirit is giving us fresh new insights into how to partner with Heaven over times and seasons. *Redeeming*

Your Timeline is going to equip you with powerful tools to get unstuck and move forward into God's timing for your life!

Jamie Galloway
Jamie Galloway Ministries
www.jamiegalloway.com
Author of *Secrets of the Seer* and others

Amazing insights and fresh revelation are what I experience every time I read or listen to Pastor Troy Brewer. The message of this book—that you can invite the redemptive power of Yeshua-Jesus into any part of your past in order to transform your present and change your future—is life changing! I am thankful for Troy for the life-changing transformational wisdom found in this book!

Rabbi Jason Sobel
Founder and CEO Fusion with Rabbi Jason

We all have unresolved pain, but as my friend Troy Brewer makes clear, Jesus is a time-traveler. He reaches into our past, transforms those hurts and uses them for His purposes. Our greatest failures can bring the greatest glory to God. This is a teaching we all need to hear. I highly recommend this book.

Jimmy Evans
Founder and CEO, MarriageToday

Redeeming Your TIMELINE

SUPERNATURAL SKILLSETS FOR HEALING PAST WOUNDS, CALMING FUTURE ANXIETIES, & DISCOVERING REST IN THE NOW

TROY A. BREWER

Dedication

This book is dedicated to my dad, William Edward "Bill" Brewer.

It has only been two months since you took your last breath of Texas air and your first breath of Heaven's. As time is relative, it has already been a long time for me to be without you.

I will see you on the Great Day when time will be no more. Until then, I will celebrate the 53 years you poured into me. Thanks for loving me, Jesus, and for finishing well.

This book is for you, dad, and for the Heavenly Father who loves us both.

 All emphasis within Scripture quotations is the author's own. Please note that Destiny Image's publishing style capitalizes certain pronouns in Scripture that refer to the Father, Son, and Holy Spirit, and may differ from some publishers' styles. Take note that the name satan and related names are not capitalized. We choose not to acknowledge him, even to the point of violating grammatical rules.

DESTINY IMAGE® PUBLISHERS, INC.
P.O. Box 310, Shippensburg, PA 17257-0310
"Promoting Inspired Lives."

This book and all other Destiny Image and Destiny Image Fiction books are available at Christian bookstores and distributors worldwide.

Cover design by Eileen Rockwell
Interior design by Terry Clifton

For more information on foreign distributors, call 717-532-3040.

Reach us on the Internet: www.destinyimage.com.

ISBN 13 TP: 978-0-7684-5400-0
ISBN 13 eBook: 978-0-7684-5401-7
ISBN 13 HC: 978-0-7684-5403-1
ISBN 13 LP: 978-0-7684-5402-4

For Worldwide Distribution, Printed in the U.S.A.
1 2 3 4 5 6 7 8 / 25 24 23 22 21

Content

Foreword

There is probably not a person alive that hasn't dealt with regret. After all, we all make mistakes. No one is perfect. This is why God being the *Great Redeemer* is such a wonderful promise. He is able to reach back into our past and not just erase the mistakes made, but redeem them and use them even for our good. This is what the scripture in Romans 8:28 so famously declares.

> *And we know that all things work together for good to those who love God, to those who are the called according to His purpose.*

We are promised that if we love God and are called in connection with His divine purpose, then all things work out for good in our future. These two prerequisites must be met however. First, we must love God. This would mean that we place Him first in our life and allow Him to be the One who gives direction and guidance to what we do. Loving God does not mean I just have some kind of warm emotion toward Him. Jesus was clear that loving God had to do with obeying His commands in John 14:15.

If you love Me, keep My commandments.

I felt the Lord say to me as I was struggling against sin one day, *"Every time you say no to your flesh, you are saying to me, 'I love you more.'"* This began to serve as a motivation to declare my love to Him through my choice to obey Him in even the smallest of places. When we truly love Him, it will propel us to obey Him. The good news is that Jesus actually works in us to bring us to this place. This is what He did with Peter when he had failed Jesus. Of course, Peter had denied the Lord. Jesus comes and ask Peter if he loves Him and will give his life for Him. Peter is destroyed and riddled with guilt in these moments. He has been uncovered and now knows his own weakness and vulnerability. He answers that he has a fond feeling for Jesus, but knows he couldn't give his life for Him. This has been manifested just a few hours earlier. Not only does Peter know this, everyone else does as well. Jesus then makes a startling statement in John 21:18-19. He promises Peter that before the process is done, He will be willing and able to give His life for Jesus without reservation.

> *"Most assuredly, I say to you, when you were younger, you girded yourself and walked where you wished; but when you are old, you will stretch out your hands, and another will gird you and carry you where you do not wish." This He spoke, signifying by what death he would glorify God. And when He had spoken this, He said to him, "Follow Me."*

Jesus would complete what He had started in Peter, just like He will complete what has been begun in us. He will bring us to such a passionate love for Himself that the joy of our hearts will be to give all to Him. He will redeem us fully to His original intent for our lives. The truth is that there is not one problem from our past that He cannot redeem. It will require, though, that we come to a place of obedience to Him to see this happen. Second Corinthians 10:6 promises us that God will punish all disobedience against us.

> *And being ready to punish all disobedience when your obedience is fulfilled.*

Notice that *when* our obedience is fulfilled that there will be a punishing of every disobedience. Among other things, this would mean that the effects of any disobedience in my life and the devil's use of it will be redeemed. God will require that anything Satan stole from me in my history because of sin, whether mine or someone else's against me, will be restored and recovered. God is able to redeem all things back. This is a result of my obedience being fulfilled that is motivated from me loving God. The other element we are told is that we must be *"called according to His purpose."* This would mean that I am living my life with the intent to complete the will of God designated to me. In other words, my passion becomes doing His will and serving His purpose in the earth rather than my own. When I lay down my own purpose and take up His purpose for my life, I enact this promise. I can expect the Lord to *work everything for my good.* This phrase implies that it will be a process. There is a *working* out in my future and a demonstrating of the goodness of God. I can expect to have a good future, because God will redeem every negative thing from my past.

We actually see this in the story where God sends the prophet Jeremiah to the potter's house in Jeremiah 18:1-6. When Jeremiah arrives at the house of the potter, he is busy with his trade.

> *The word which came to Jeremiah from the Lord, saying: "Arise and go down to the potter's house, and there I will cause you to hear My words." Then I went down to the potter's house, and there he was, making something at the wheel. And the vessel that he made of clay was marred in the hand of the potter; so he made it again into another vessel, as it seemed good to the potter to make.*
>
> *Then the word of the Lord came to me, saying: "O house of Israel, can I not do with you as this potter?" says the Lord. "Look, as the clay is in the potter's hand, so are you in My hand, O house of Israel!"*

The Lord uses the natural event of a potter making a vessel to speak to Jeremiah about the nation of Israel. He lets Jeremiah know that He is the potter and the people of the nation are the clay. Just like the vessel naturally in the potter's hand became marred and blemished, so had Israel become in the hand of God. Notice that when the vessel was being made and it became marred, the potter didn't throw it away and get another piece of clay. He was committed to this piece of clay and its usefulness. He simply turned it into another vessel. The Lord is absolutely faithful to us. He doesn't give up on us. Even when we give up on ourselves, He stays true. He will finish what He has started. The marring of the vessel was a result of the deficiency in the clay, not a reflection on the ability or character of the potter. Any marring of our lives is not because God didn't love us or because He didn't care for us. The marring was because of sin. Sin was imbedded in us. It was a part of our nature. It caused the marring of our lives. God however doesn't throw us away and get another piece of clay. He simply turns us into another vessel. He actually leaves the imperfections in the clay and through His perfection, weaves them into the finished product. In other words, the brokenness of our past when redeemed, becomes a part of our story that makes us who we are. As the Master Potter, the Lord is able to perfect that which concerns us. He is not offended at our struggles. He, in fact, will use our struggles to make us unique and special in His sight. The pain of our past when healed will be woven into our future. We will be a demonstration of the grace and goodness of the Lord. We become trophies of His grace who carry a special sense of destiny and purpose created by and through Him and His abilities toward us. Only one thing is required, that we stay on the potter's wheel. The potter's wheel goes round and round. Perhaps you seem to be going in circles, never getting anywhere. This could be a season where the Lord is forming you as the Master Potter. We must in these times not get frustrated and get off the wheel. We must stay on the wheel and let patience have its perfect work according to James 1:4.

> *But let patience have its perfect work, that you may be perfect and complete, lacking nothing.*

As we allow the Lord our Potter to fashion us, we will come to a place of completeness, perfection and missing nothing. The Lord is faithful to fulfill His word.

In this book *Redeeming Your Timeline*, my friend Troy Brewer unveils powerful and significant principles to seeing what I have just described occur. No matter where you have come from, the future that God has for you is unfathomable. This is what we are promised in First Corinthians 2:9. These words might seem impossible for some, yet they are the promise and assertion of God Himself.

> *But as it is written:*
> *"Eye has not seen, nor ear heard,*
> *Nor have entered into the heart of man*
> *The things which God has prepared for those who love Him."*

This simply means that you have not yet fully imagined what God has planned for your life. He is working all things for your good. Anything in your past that might seem to taint or corrupt this, God is able to redeem. I exhort you to please take this book and let God use it to recover your history. He is the Lord of the past, present, and future. Nothing is too hard or difficult for Him. He will grant you the future you may have not even yet seen.

Robert Henderson
Bestselling Author, *Courts of Heaven Series*

Introduction

Hopefully, you heard about this book and had to check it out for yourself. Thank you for having the courage to do that. You are a busy person and your time could be spent doing anything right now. I don't want to waste it.

As we will discover together, *time is a big deal.*

I promise to do my very best to bring you a revelation of how awesome Jesus is in a way that is fun, real, and relevant to you right where you are. I tend to judge books by the effect they have on my life. I encourage you to do the same with this one.

> This book is for people who love supernatural power and aspire to be a hope fanatic.

This book is for people who love transformation and those hungry few who dare to say no to the cages they crave. This book is for people who love supernatural power and aspire to be a hope fanatic. This book is for normal people who want more than normal outcomes in their lives. If you are somebody who loves it when Kingdom people win no matter what, and you are not afraid to get out of the box, this book is for you.

I am going to warn you though, it comes with challenges to your heart and to your willingness to see through a very different lens. How you see your own timeline is going to change—that is the space between your birth day and the last date on your memorial.

Redeeming Time

We are also going to discover that redemption is a big deal. If there is no redemption, then time is nothing but a slow death to all creation. If you make a big deal out of time, you have to make a big deal out of redemption—and we are going to do that in a really big way.

We are going to discover how time works, what God crafted time for, and how He moves in and out of time on behalf of His people.

Don't let the whole time thing or the whole redemption thing scare you. By the time you finish this book, you will have a great understanding of how they intersect in your life, and how much hope this revelation will bring to even the darkest of memories or fears for your future.

If you don't consider yourself a quantum theorist or didn't sit at the front of the smart row in elementary school, keep reading.

This book and the revelational conclusion we will come to, is really not just about time. It is actually about being set free. Time doesn't have to own you and you do not have to be chained to your past in any way at all. You are no more chained to your time than you are to the chair you are sitting in or the real estate you're standing on.

Prerequisites, Premises, and Lines of Logic

Among the many strange ideas about this revelation, we are going to make sure we have the foundations right. Now, in order for us to get to the conclusion of this truth that will set you free, we are going to spend time on several premises.

A premise is when you follow a line of logic that will support a conclusion. Basically, it's the things you have to know to come to the revelation. The Bible would call it a "therefore."

> A premise is when you follow a line of logic that will support a conclusion.

It's like when Jesus says, "OK. Now that you understand that idea, from there we move forward." The Bible is loaded with "therefores." There are a titanic 1,220 "therefores" throughout the entire Bible—76 in the book of John alone!

> *If the Son therefore shall make you free, ye shall be free indeed.*
>
> —John 8:36

> *He that is of God heareth God's words: ye therefore hear them not, because ye are not of God.*
>
> —John 8:47

So, in the spirit of '76, we learn to be set free. Therefore, in the Bible, a premise is kind of like saying, "OK. Now that you understand that, you can go on to understand this."

There will be some of that in this book. I will present several propositions supporting and leading you to a certain conclusion.

You do not have to be caged by your past or fearful of your future.

What's the conclusion? What's this world-changing and life-altering revelation?

It's simple. You do not have to be caged by your past or fearful of your future. You can invite Jesus Christ into your past or your future, and His redemptive power can change everything in your now.

I have devoted a segment to each groundbreaking truth where we will unpack these Kingdom ideas. They look like this:

Premise 1—God created time. He is not subject or shackled by it in any way.

Premise 2—God created time for the purpose of works of redemption.

Premise 3—Redemption changes everything.

Premise 4—You can introduce redemption into any part of your timeline and it changes everything within the timeline, including space and matter.

Premise 5—We are stewards—not owners—of our lives. As priests, we apply the blood. As kings, we bring Kingdom dominion into all we steward, including time.

Conclusion: We can bring the redemptive power of the cross into any moment in our past and it will set us free right in the right now. We can also invite Jesus into our future, which will position us for His hopeful outcome—right now.

Jesus is a time traveler. We can partner with Him for His presence—His redeeming blood—to be made manifest in every moment of our lives. Chains in our current situation will fall off when we displace the enemy in our past with His manifest presence.

Included with these chapters are exercises and testimonies. I encourage you to take time to learn how time works, and how time can work for you. Learn the powerful, prophetic act of redeeming time and be set free right now, and in your future, from things that have happened in your past.

Jesus is a time traveler.

You do not have to be a slave to your past. Your destiny is greater than your history when Jesus steps in.

Jesus Christ is called the One who was, the One who is, and the One who is yet to come (see Revelation 1:8). Wait until you find out how to know Him in all three of those places at once. This is going to be fun!

—Troy

My favorite things in life don't cost any money. It's really clear that the most precious resource we all have is time.

—Steve Jobs

Section One

WHAT IS TIME?

Understanding the Makeup of the Created Thing Called "Time"

PREMISE 1

God created time and is not subject or shackled by it in any way.

In this section you will learn about:

- The created continuum of time, space, and matter.
- The relative power of redeemed time.
- The relative power of unredeemed time.
- The dominion of actions in linear timelines.
- The prophetic layers of cyclical timelines.
- The river and flow of time.
- The prophetic Issachar anointing.
- The position of the heart determines our view of time.

- The different kinds of created time.
- The epic eras of what the Bible calls "times."
- The predictable cycles of what the Bible calls "seasons."

1

The Hands of Time

If you have been around for any amount of time, you know time is a common part of everyday, expressive language. We say things like:

- "In the nick of time"— meaning just before time ran out.
- "Time flies"—meaning accelerated time.
- "Time marches on"—which says something about unstoppable time.
- "Time on my hands"—which might mean wasted time or a feeling of more than enough time.
- "A stitch in time" talks about disciplined time.
- "Time out" is all about stopping the clock.
- "Time in" talks of restarting the clock and becoming rededicated to the game.
- "Passing time" speaks of leisurely waiting.
- "Doing time" is a prison term.

- "Killing time" could also be called spending time, or wasting it.
- "Wasting time" is a lot like killing time.
- "Losing time" is connected to the anxiety of running out of time.
- "On time" means "as scheduled."
- "For the time being" means right now, but things could change.
- "Big time" means super important or influential.
- "The time of your life" speaks of dreams coming true.
- And "once upon a time" is a poetic term for a past time frame, either real or imagined.

Just today, I have noted phrases like "Time is critical," "Time is crucial," "It's about time," and I heard the phrase, "Time is money" twice.

Oh, we are all about time! But, do we really know what time even is?

This is my worldview of time: Time is a gift from God.

God gave you time.

Time is something that can be measured, numbered, and predicted by common people. Time is an environment that God created for our safety and sanity. We need to understand time in order to partner with His purposes for us because time is the place where purpose is accomplished and transformation takes place.

> *To everything there is a season, and a time to every purpose under the heaven.*
>
> —Ecclesiastes 3:1

Time has the kiss of God for His people and the sharp teeth of mortality for the unbelieving and hard of heart. Time is a blessing for the redeemed and a curse for God's haters. It owns everything that isn't Kingdom. It is a valuable tool for the purposes of the redeemed and the Redeemer. Scripture tells us God gives and God takes away (Job 1:21). When it comes to time, we need to know the prophetic value of time before we step into eternity. Let's unpack this.

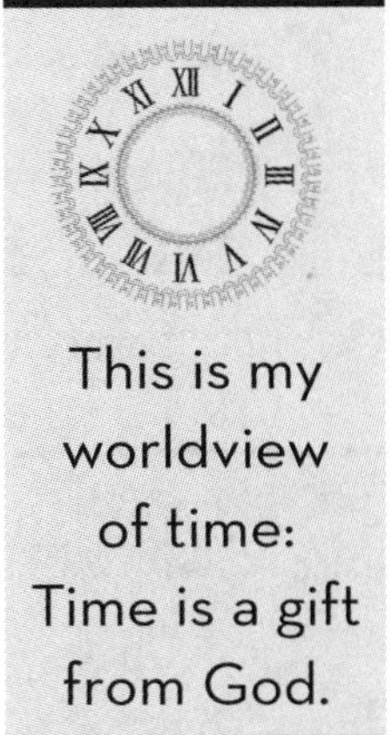

This is my worldview of time: Time is a gift from God.

Hammer Time

I played guitar in a Christian rock band throughout the late 1980s. Many times, we played secular sets in bars and clubs because we didn't want to starve to death. We also used it as a powerful outreach to the rock community. We purposefully chose songs with Kingdom themes. Some of my favorites were "Long Train Running" by the Doobie Brothers and "Caught in the Crossfire" by Stevie Ray Vaughn.

At the end of the night, we would let everybody know we were Christians and offer to share Jesus with them in the parking lot or over at the bar.

One night in Austin, Texas, I was playing on world-famous 6th Street at a place called The Liberty Lunch. In the middle of praying for a young married couple sitting at the bar, I looked up and saw a framed statement that changed by life. It was among pictures of crop duster airplanes, guitar players, and Texas folk art. The framed quote read:

> Time is God's way of keeping everything from happening at once.

I didn't know it at the time, but that was actually a quote from Einstein. I had to drive all the way back to Johnson County, Texas, and I couldn't get that phrase out of my head. I prayed out loud and asked God, "Sir, why wouldn't You want everything to happen at one time?"

Time is God's way of keeping everything from happening at once

That night, God began to talk to me about time in an ongoing dialogue that is still in conversation today.

It turns out, God wants us to move from past to future, from dark to light, and from death to life. He likes progression and forward movement. If He is going to redeem us and move us from history to destiny, time is the only place something like that can happen. Time is a stage where the spotlight can shine on redemption and transformation.

The **BIG** Headline from Chapter 1

Time is a gift from God. Within the time He gives us is the package of purpose and opportunity through relationship. He doesn't allow everything to happen at once because He has more value for relationship and redemption than for functionality and punishment. Everything in the Kingdom is relational before it is functional.

God could have had you born into your fulfilled ultimate destiny, but He chose to develop relationship with you. Poof! You could have been suddenly there in highest heaven, crowned and robed in His righteousness—and you might wonder what happened, or worse, be totally unprepared for what is about to take place. If God didn't love having relationship with you He could just say, "Trust Me, I played it all out and this is how it would have ended up." But He loves you so much, He took the formidable risk and the terrible pain of all the things that happen in the history of humanity upon Himself.

What This Means to You

Because you have time, you have a great opportunity to grow with Him and in Him. In the time frame you have been trusted with, you have an opening to achieve the impossible and fulfill the purpose of actually being an ambassador of heaven. Time is your ticket to personally see God change everything with you, for you, and through you. As long as you have time, you still have hope.

> *With long life I will satisfy him, and show him My salvation.*
>
> —Psalm 91:16

Questions to Ponder

Since God created time for your benefit, how can you better partner with God in hope and joy?

Do you see time as a gift from God? Why or why not? How does your view of time need to be different now?

2

God's Eye on Time

Let's look at how the Bible introduces heaven's view of time.

God's Glory in Time

I want to take you back to an ancient setting. Moses, the Jew who didn't belong in the house of the Egyptians and wasn't welcome in the camp of his own people, had run away and lived with another group he didn't belong to. After forty years of time, he finally found somebody he belonged to—God.

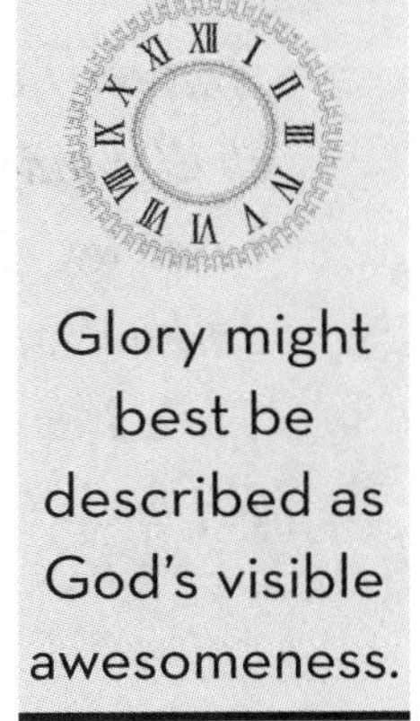

Glory might best be described as God's visible awesomeness.

After a world-famous supernatural showdown with Pharaoh, the most powerful man on the planet, Moses wanted a deeper walk with God. God granted this man, His friend, a request, and Moses went for it, saying, *"Show me your glory"* (Exodus 33:18). He wanted to see the "glory" of God. Glory might best be described as God's visible awesomeness. Otherwise hidden from people who do not have a heart to truly know Him, Moses was like Oliver Twist. He dared to ask for more.

The relationship Moses had with God was special. So was the revelation God had for him. Upon request, God replied that His awesomeness would not be seen head-on. But, still, He had a plan and we find it in Exodus chapter 33:

> *So the Lord said to Moses, "I will also do this thing that you have spoken; for you have found grace in My sight, and I know you by name."*
>
> *And he* [Moses] *said, "Please, show me Your glory."*
>
> *Then He said, "I will make all My goodness pass before you, and I will proclaim the name of the Lord before you. I will be gracious to whom I will be gracious, and I will have compassion on whom I will have compassion." But He said, "You cannot see My face; for no man shall see Me, and live."*
>
> *And the Lord said, "Here is a place by Me, and you shall stand on the rock. So it shall be, while My glory passes by, that I will put you in the cleft of the rock, and will cover you with My hand while I pass by. Then I will take away My hand, and you shall see My back; but My face shall not be seen."*
>
> —Exodus 33:17-23

A time long ago, Moses went to the top of the mountain and saw the backside of God. In a tiny glimpse of God's glory through the lens of redemption, Moses saw the goodness of God from that moment backward in *time past.* All of it! Every good thing God had done and every good way God had been in the past, I believe Moses saw it all in a game-changing glimpse of God's backside.

You might not know it, but this is a reference to a timeline. Everything under the law deals with present/past tense, so this is the way God revealed His glory, or visible awesomeness, to Moses—in present/past tense.

So, when Moses put his ancient feather to the animal skin canvas, these were the epic words he would introduce to the world as the written Word of God:

> *In the beginning God created the heavens and the earth.*
>
> —Genesis 1:1

That is how he starts off the Bible. An ancient, barefoot man in the Middle East comes down from a mountain with a reference to God creating time, space, and matter all at once.

Everything under the law deals with present/past tense.

From Here to Eternity

Today, modern science describes space-time as "a mathematical model that joins space and time into a single idea called a continuum." *When something is in "continuum," it means if the one exists, then the other exists.* Or, if you get rid of the one thing, you have to get rid of the other. That's how it is with time and space, or you could also say time and distance.

Also in continuum with space and time, is matter. This simply means that time, space, and matter are connected in a way that makes them inseparable, and that's what Genesis 1 actually says!

> *In the beginning* [time] *God created the heavens* [space] *and the earth* [matter].
>
> —Genesis 1:1

Time and creation are connected. Time is a created thing.

This amazing truth was written for the world to see 3,500 years before Albert Einstein or Hermann Minkowski first suggested a space-time continuum in 1908. Before these two Jews brought this truth to the world, another Jew 35 centuries earlier put it in black and white.

So, the Bible begins by letting us know God is not subject to time, space, or matter. However, time, and all that's in continuum with it including human beings, are subject to Him because He is the Creator of those things.

At this point, time and creation are connected. Time is a created thing. Time was created by God and actually serves God's very specific purposes. Because there are different purposes of God, He has created different kinds of time to fulfill those purposes.

> *To everything there is a season, a time for every purpose under heaven.*
>
> —Ecclesiastes 3:1

The BIG Headline from Chapter 2

When you see time through the lens of God's goodness as Moses did, you see God's creative genius and heart for purpose. You also see that with His intention for the fulfillment of certain outcomes, He creates environments and places for them to actually happen. Time is a created environment that He places space and matter in. Heaven and earth both have timelines with beginning and end; however, our Creator does not.

What This Means to You

If you can wrap your head around this first premise—that God created time, space, and matter to work together for your good and His purposes—you can be introduced to limitless possibilities that will certainly set you free. This key creates a powerful entry through Kingdom doorways to all places in your timeline. Because He has dominion over all He has created, God has easy access to your past and future.

If God is not subject to time, then God is not subject to any circumstance, past, present, or future in your timeline. Every failure and shameful flaw can be targeted by redemption from the Redeemer who can step into any time frame.

> *For thus says the High and Lofty One who inhabits eternity, whose name is Holy: "I dwell in the high and holy place, with him who has a contrite and humble spirit, to revive the spirit of the humble, and to revive the heart of the contrite ones."*
>
> —Isaiah 57:15

Questions to Ponder

Pastor Troy believes Moses saw history past when God showed him His "backside" and this is where Moses received the revelation for the book of Genesis. What do you think of this premise?

How does the revelation of the time-space continuum in Genesis 1:1 change the way you think of creation? The way you think of time?

What do you think God's purpose for time is?

3

What God Can Do with His Creation Called Time

Time is one of the most amazing features of all God's creation. Just like the rest of God's creation, Jesus Christ rules and reigns over all of it.

> *In the beginning was the Word, and the Word was with God, and the Word was God. He was in the beginning with God. All things were made through Him, and without Him nothing was made that was made.*
>
> —John 1:1-3

Before He came to earth as the man Jesus, the Bible says His name in eternity was "the Word." According to this Scripture passage, Jesus can put His hands on time because God (the Word) spoke the universe into existence.

> *Ah, Sovereign LORD, you have made the heavens and the earth by your great power and by outstretched arm. Nothing is too hard for you.*
>
> —Jeremiah 32:17 NIV

He can also order time.

> *For God is not a God of disorder, but of peace—as in all the congregations of the Lord's people.*
>
> —1 Corinthians 14:33 NIV

He can stop time.

> *So the sun stood still, and the moon stopped, till the nation avenged itself on its enemies....*
>
> —Joshua 10:13 NIV

He can accelerate time.

> *...the plowman shall overtake the reaper....*
>
> —Amos 9:13

He can change time.

> *I will make the shadow cast by the sun go back the ten steps it has gone down on the stairway of Ahaz.*
>
> —Isaiah 38:8 NIV

He can change space and distance because it is in continuum with time.

> *Now when they came up out of the water, the Spirit of the Lord caught Philip away, so that the eunuch*

> *saw him no more; and he went on his way rejoicing. But Philip was found at Azotus....*
>
> —Acts 8:39-40

He can change matter just like when Jesus turned water into wine and healed people of leprosy. Again, time, space, and matter, though different, are totally inseparable.

He can even step in and out of time anywhere He chooses as easily as you or I can step on or off a train anywhere along the line of a track.

If you can believe God can be with somebody on the other side of the world at the same time He is with you, then it is not much of a leap to believe He can step into your past, even though He is with you right now, because space and time are in continuum.

You might need to think about this for minute.

It doesn't take any more faith for you to believe God can step into your past or your future right now, than it does to believe God can heal the sick, because time and matter are also in continuum.

The same God who can make cancer disappear because of His redeeming power can also redeem your timeline and cause a terrible thing that happened to you become nothing more than a bump in the road.

It might seem impossible, but God changing your darkness into noonday is not just a poetic expression. It's a declaration of His dominion over your time frame. (See Isaiah 58:10.)

So, all of the systems of time, for God, are like the weather, or world governments or human bodies. He has designed it to run according to certain principles and laws. However, He can step into any single time frame and change it the same as He can heal a human body, reroute a hurricane, or unseat a demonic king.

Time, space, and matter are part of God's creation and in perfect continuum. If you believe God can go into your future and prepare the way, you can also be confident He can go into your past and redeem actions and events there. As soon as you lock into this revelation, you are on your way to redeeming time in a way that affects your "right now."

> He can step into any single time frame and change it the same as He can heal a human body, reroute a hurricane, or unseat a demonic king.

Time is created by God and time is in every way subject to God's authority. That's the bottom line.

The **BIG** Headline from Chapter 3

Premise 1:

- Time is created by God.
- Time is subject to God. God is not subject to time.

That's the bottom line. There is nothing God cannot do, with or through time. He made it. He owns it. He changes it and makes it work for Him and His purposes.

What This Means to You

If you believe God can heal somebody of leprosy, you can believe God can change matter. Same as if you believe He can turn water into wine or raise a dead body to life. If that is true—and it is—and if it is true that time and matter are inseparable—and it is—then you can also believe the following: God can change your time from a diseased timeline into a healthy timeline because time and matter are in perfect continuum.

If God can be into two places at once, He can be in two different timelines at once. Again, you cannot separate time from distance or space.

I am not saying you are a time traveler. I am saying that God certainly is and we will talk more about that in a bit. It's impossible for you to change time, but it certainly isn't for God.

> *But He said, "The things which are impossible with men are possible with God."*
>
> —Luke 18:27

Questions to Ponder

God is the Creator of time and Scripture shows He has the power to manipulate it. What Scriptures can you think of where God changed time?

Why do you think God would change time? Who do you think He would change time for?

Do you believe Jesus is a time traveler? Why? What evidence is there in Scripture?

4

Different Kinds of Time

What we are about to learn is that God has made different kinds of time the way He had made different kinds of trees, flowers, or really anything. We love dogs, but there are different kinds of dogs and time is just like that. *All kinds of time are created for different purposes.*

> *To everything there is a season, a time for every purpose under heaven.*
>
> —Ecclesiastes 3:1

Because there are different kinds of time for different purposes of God, there is no telling how many kinds of time there are, but let's start off with some easy ones.

Past time:

Time gone by and no longer existing (from our perspective), or something occurring before, and leading up to, the time of right now.

Present time:

I call this "right now" time and, again, all of this is relative to each human being.

Future time:

A later time from your "right now" time.

Because we are human and uniquely created, we deal with our past, present, and our futures differently.

So, we know there are different kinds of time. So far, it's been easy. Now, the Bible begins to show us other kinds of time.

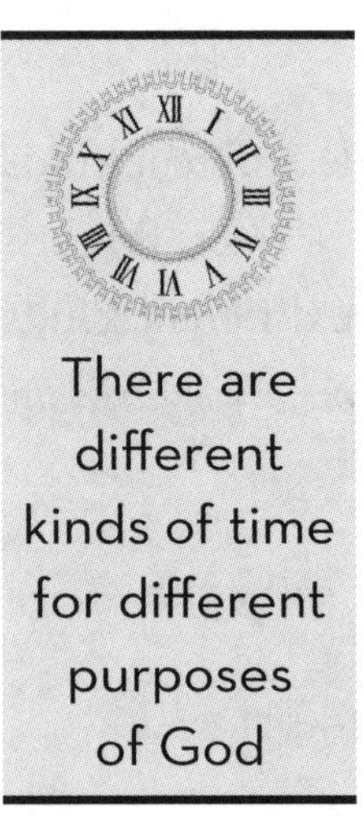

There are different kinds of time for different purposes of God

Unredeemed time:

A flow of relative time when everything is being lost and passing away.

When redemption is not at work and the blood of the Lamb is absent, time is a robber and a destroyer. Time is death and a prison. Entropy rules in unredeemed time. Disorder, uncertainty, and degradation show up and make sure that humans have no strength or ability to exercise authority.

In unredeemed time, the focus is on what is being lost and what is passing away. This is the state of the world where something scientists call "entropy" is engaged. *Entropy is a law of thermodynamic physics. Lack of order or predictability always leads to a gradual decline into disorder.*

This is what happens when nature rules and reigns, and when the Creator does not. In its natural designed state, time, without the rule of heaven or the component of redemption, is designed to guarantee a continual ending.

Here are some Bible verses that illustrate entropy in unredeemed time frames:

> *And when midday was past, they prophesied until the time of the offering of the evening sacrifice. But there was no voice; no one answered, no one paid attention.*
>
> —1 Kings 18:29

Do you see how the Bible describes the time frame? It's going away or passing. In the Doppler effect, they would say it's in redshift.

> *Oh, that You would hide me in the grave, that You would conceal me until Your wrath is past, that You would appoint me a set time, and remember me!*
>
> —Job 14:13

> *Envy, murders, drunkenness, revelries, and the like; of which I tell you beforehand, just as I also told you in time past, that those who practice such things will not inherit the kingdom of God.*
>
> —Galatians 5:21

> *God, who at various times and in various ways spoke in time past to the fathers by the prophets, has in these last days spoken to us by His Son, whom He*

> *has appointed heir of all things, through whom also He made the worlds.*
>
> —Hebrews 1:1-2

Do you see the difference between "time past" and "in these last days"? Everything in unredeemed time is fading away.

> *Woe to the crown of pride, to the drunkards of Ephraim, whose glorious beauty is a fading flower which is at the head of the verdant valleys, to those who are overcome with wine!*
>
> —Isaiah 28:1

Everything caught up in the flow of unredeemed time is forced to fade and pass away. That's the purpose of unredeemed time.

> *And the world is passing away, and the lust of it; but he who does the will of God abides forever.*
>
> —1 John 2:17

It reminds me of the last words of Frank Sinatra, "I'm losing it. I'm losing it!" The state of what I call "unredeemed time" makes sure that death brings an ending. This is because space, time, and matter are also in continuum with sin and death, but we will get into that in another chapter.

We are all very familiar with unredeemed time. However, there is another side of time to discover.

I don't know if Frank Sinatra was redeemed or not. I'm merely talking about what kind of time he was dealing with when he died. I can tell you that the apostle Paul wasn't losing anything. He was actually gaining everything. Why? Time was different for him because of redemption.

> *For to me, to live is Christ, and to die is gain.*
>
> —PHILIPPIANS 1:21

And that brings us to redeemed time.

Redeemed time:

A flow of relative time where everything is coming and being gained. When the blood of the Lamb is present, the rules are completely different for that specific time frame. It's the difference between coming or going. In redeemed time, the person in that time flow is gaining life instead of losing life. Time serves God in bringing and giving instead of passing and taking away.

Everything caught up in the flow of unredeemed time is forced to fade and pass away.

Here are some good biblical examples:

> *Your kingdom come. Your will be done on earth as it is in heaven.*
>
> —MATTHEW 6:10

> *But when thefullness of the time had come, God sent forth His Son, born of a woman, born under the law.*
>
> —GALATIANS 4:4

> *Then Samuel said to the people, "Come, let us go to Gilgal and renew the kingdom there."*
>
> —1 SAMUEL 11:14

> *When your days are fulfilled and you rest with your fathers, I will set up your seed after you, who will come from your body, and I will establish his kingdom.*
>
> —2 Samuel 7:12

> *Then the King will say to those on His right hand, "Come, you blessed of My Father, inherit the kingdom prepared for you from the foundation of the world."*
>
> —Matthew 25:34

> *Blessed is the kingdom of our father David that comes in the name of the Lord! Hosanna in the highest!*
>
> —Mark 11:10

> *And heal the sick there, and say to them, "The kingdom of God has come near to you."*
>
> —Luke 10:9

Important Note

In the flow of redeemed time, all things of the Kingdom and life are coming. The presence of God continues to come more and more in the flow of redeemed time. It's a lot like when Isaiah saw the train of the glory of God in chapter 6:1: *"I saw the Lord sitting on a throne, high and lifted up, and the train of His robe filled the temple."* The Hebrew word we translate as "filled" the temple actually means "to fill and continue to fill more and more." It's a perfect picture of what happens when His holy presence and His redemption enters into a certain time frame.

On the other hand, in the flow of unredeemed time, all things of the world are passing away, fading and dying.

As we will discover in another chapter, time is proven to be relative, especially to the observer. Your view of time is determined by the condition of your heart and the authority you walk in or the victimization you are burdened with.

Your timeline is subject, or relative to, how you are able to observe it—whether through the view of heaven or through what the Bible calls an evil eye.

> *The light of the body is the eye: if therefore your eye be single, thy whole body shall be full of light. But if thine eye be evil, thy whole body shall be full of darkness....*
>
> —Matthew 6:22-23 KJV

In the flow of redeemed time, all things of the Kingdom and life are coming

You can literally change everything by changing your view from a natural view to a redeemed and supernatural view. That means seeing your time through Him and His awesome glory. He causes His goodness to pass before you and you see through that amazing lens of relationship. You can change your time from robbing you into adding life to you. This is the way God designed time. He designed it for you to walk in it in a way that is relative to your heart and your relationship with Him.

Messing with time is a lot like flying a jet or driving a race car. You had better know what model you are dealing with. We have to learn to partner with God so redeemed time can overtake our past, present, and future time.

Redeemed time and unredeemed are both time. Just like a Labrador and a wild wolf are both dogs. We have to know how to enjoy the benefits of the one while overcoming the other.

> *See then that you walk circumspectly, not as fools but as wise, redeeming the time, because the days are evil.*
>
> —Ephesians 5:15-16

The BIG Headline from Chapter 4

When redemption is at work, time is completely different from when redemption is not at work within that time.

When the blood of the Lamb is absent, time is a robber and a destroyer. Time is death and a prison. Entropy rules in unredeemed time.

When redemption enters, time becomes a transformational environment from death unto life. Maturity, fruitfulness, dreams realized, goals achieved, and prayers answered become the norm. Heaven comes to you in a time frame shifted by redemption.

What This Means to You

Not only do you need to be aware of your past, present, and future, you need to be aware of the redeemed and "yet to be redeemed" places in your timeline. There are places in your timeline where the King needs to bring redemption. In bad places, He changes the curse to a blessing. In good places, you continue to receive the Kingdom and His goodness without losing it.

> *He has made everything beautiful in its time. Also He has put eternity in their hearts, except that no one can find out the work that God does from beginning to end.*
>
> —ECCLESIASTES 3:11

Questions to Ponder

How is time relative in my life?

In my own words, what is the difference between redeemed and unredeemed time?

Do I believe redeemed time is available to me? If so, what events in my life would I like to see redeemed?

5

Time Lines and Time Circles

On the menu are some other kinds of time to taste. Let me introduce to you two others you might not be familiar with: *linear and cyclical timelines* also known as *times and seasons.*

There is a difference between time lines and time circles. Cyclical timelines in the Bible are actually called seasons, and they are always prophetic.

The twelve signs in the Zodiac—or the Mazzaroth as the Bible calls it in Job 38:31-32 and Second Kings 23:3-5—encircle the earth and a new sign comes up every month. As noted in my book *Looking Up,* the signs prophesy and tell us exactly how God will redeem His people. Since this story is prophetic, it's in a circle.

> *Its rising is from one end of heaven, and its circuit to the other end; and there is nothing hidden from its heat* [passion].
>
> —Psalm 19:6

When you know which sign is up this month, you know which sign is up next month. It's predictable because it is prophetic. It has a circuit.

When you are in fall, you know winter is coming and so on. It's a cycle and it is supposed to be predictable. Again, this falls into prophetic categories.

In that same way of thinking, you can't help but notice when prophets move in the Bible, they move in circles.

> *And Samuel judged Israel all the days of his life. He went up from year to year on a circuit to Bethel, Gilgal, and Mizpah, and judged Israel in all those places. But he always returned to Ramah, for his home was there. There he judged Israel, and there he built an altar to the LORD.*
>
> —1 Samuel 7:15-17

When Jesus moved in circuits, they were actually prophetic acts. The Holman Christian Standard Bible translates Mark 6:6 this way:

> *And He was amazed at their unbelief. Now He was going around the villages in a circuit, teaching.*

The King James Bible version calls it "round about."

However you want to say it, Jesus was in alignment for His prophetic assignment by acting in circular patterns in how He physically carried out His prophetic ministry.

He causes prophetic time to do the same. Rotate.

So, what we are talking about are the kinds of time known as times and seasons. One is a line and the other is a circle. One is the new thing (times) and the other is the next thing (seasons).

There is a supernatural, God-given ability to discern your times and seasons so you can cooperate with God. You have to know the difference.

I call it the Issachar anointing. Because Issachar is a tribe of Israel, it is a tribal anointing. Tribal anointings are released through the people you intentionally live life with. Just like all the biblical giant slayers are people who lived life with David. Prophetic community is essential when it comes to the Issachar anointing.

> *The sons* [of the tribe] *of Issachar who had understanding of the times, to know what Israel ought to do....*
>
> —1 Chronicles 12:32

One is the new thing *(times)* and the other is the next thing *(seasons).*

Prophetically, you know *when* before you know *what* because the when determines the what. The time is created for the purpose. The time tells you what to do and how to posture yourself. God designed times like this because knowing the when determines what action you take.

Knowing what to do flows out of a full understanding of what season you are in. Blessed people understand times and seasons—natural and supernatural.

> *Who then is a faithful and wise servant, whom his master made ruler over his household, to give them*

> *food in due season? Blessed is that servant whom his master, when he comes, will find so doing.*
>
> —Matthew 24:45-46

The wisdom of God (being a wise servant) and spiritual authority (ruling his own house) are specifically related to flowing with the Spirit from season to season.

Daniel knew that.

> *Daniel answered and said, Blessed be the name of God for ever and ever: for wisdom and might are his: And he changeth the times and the seasons: he removeth kings, and setteth up kings: he giveth wisdom unto the wise, and knowledge to them that know understanding: He revealeth the deep and secret things: he knoweth what is in the darkness, and the light dwelleth with him.*
>
> —Daniel 2:20-22 KJV

Even though he was not a happy camper, Solomon was still a powerful prophet.

God changes the times and the seasons. He removes kings and sets up kings.

In different seasons, you are given different authority.

King Solomon knew something about what time is and how it works. He wrote a very strange prophetic book and included some of his insight. The book of Ecclesiastes is a mysterious book written almost 3,000 years ago. There were less than 100 million people on the planet and there were only a few languages, yet from this tiny, ancient Middle Eastern country comes something supernaturally amazing and it has to do with times and seasons.

The name Ecclesiastes is derived from the Greek word *ekklesia* (assembly) and means "one who addresses an assembly." In Hebrew it means "one who convenes an assembly." It basically means everybody has to listen to me and pay attention to what I am telling them.

Ecclesiastes is generally credited to Solomon and it would have been written in his old age. He wrote the Song of Solomon when he was young and full of passion. He wrote Proverbs in his wisdom as a middle-aged man and anointed king. It could be said that by the time Solomon wrote Ecclesiastes, he was a rude dude in crude mood.

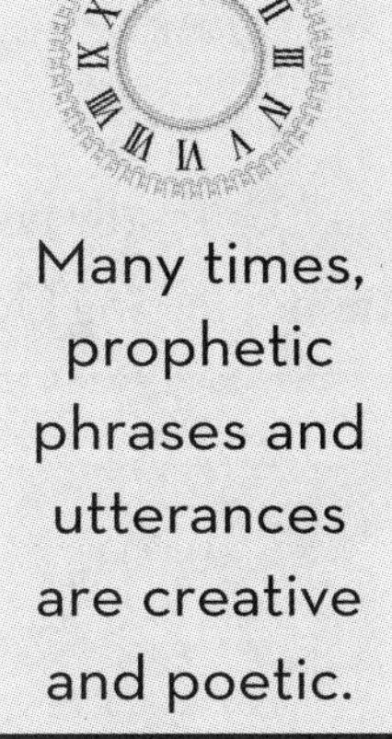
Many times, prophetic phrases and utterances are creative and poetic.

Like a lot of people, Solomon didn't finish well and he was generally unhappy about a lot of things in life. However, this book is not all pessimistic. Even though he was not a happy camper, Solomon was still a powerful prophet.

In the third chapter of this ancient book, there is a rotational prophetic timeline that has mostly been dismissed as poetry. It is poetic because it's actually prophetic. Many times, prophetic phrases and utterances are creative and poetic. Solomon got that from his daddy, King David.

In Ecclesiastes chapter 3, he starts off this prophetic calendar by saying, *"To everything there is a season, and a time to every purpose under the heaven."*

There are four ideas we are mapping out here—times and seasons; timing and purpose. It is a big curse to be out of timing. In Deuteronomy 28, Moses describes the out-of-timing curse like this:

> *Your life shall hang in doubt before you; you shall fear day and night, and have no assurance of life. In the morning you shall say, "Oh, that it were evening!" And at evening you shall say, "Oh, that it were morning!"*
>
> —Deuteronomy 28:66-67

You're always out of sync and your timing is off when you are not letting God be God. And when your timing is off, you're at the wrong place at the wrong time and the wrong things happen.

Times are epic prophetic moments that bring definition to things.

When you're out of sync, you are fighting the wrong battles and standing on the wrong battlefields. The Kingdom's answer to the curse of bad timing is to flow with the Holy Spirit through times of seasons.

Let's unpack this.

I believe we have a tremendous responsibility to understand the times and the seasons we are in. We should ask God to prophetically reveal His plans and commands for this day, ready to carry out our marching orders.

Times and Seasons are Different

Times and seasons speak of different prophetic time frames and postures.

Times

Times are epic prophetic moments that bring definition to things. They are epic moments and events that stop old things and begin new things.

When you enter into a new time, you enter into a new era. A new wine (move of God) requiring a new wine skin (priorities and culture).

> *And no one puts new wine into old wineskins; or else the new wine bursts the wineskins, the wine is spilled, and the wineskins are ruined. But new wine must be put into new wineskins.*
>
> —Mark 2:22

When you enter into the new era of what the Bible calls a time, you have to be willing to wrap your head around the new thing and think differently.

> *Behold, I will do a new thing, now it shall spring forth; shall you not know it?*
>
> —Isaiah 43:19

Again, the kind of time called "times" speaks of epic, defining events that serve as prophetic markers. Our actions have to be conformed to this so times are to be coordinated with actions. There was the time this happened or the time that event happened. There are always beginning and ending markers.

With a new time comes a cutoff from the last time, but with a new season comes a handoff to the next season.

Seasons

Seasons speak of prophetic appointments.

Prophetic appointments have to do with where you meet God and what the theme of your meeting is all about. It's why there are certain feasts in certain seasons that are celebrated with certain Kingdom themes.

Seasons speak of prophetic appointments

The theme narrative is a subject, a topic, maybe a burden or a message. When it comes to seasons, you know the when and you know the what. Every time you meet God in that certain place at that certain time, He offers a new layer of revelation on the subject. You align your confessions, proclamations, and declarations that go with this prophetic season for your life.

This is all about something I call "Alignment for Assignment."

Some biblical examples of specific seasons for wonderful things to happen could include a predictable or due season of reaping:

> *And let us not be weary in well doing: for in due season we shall reap, if we faint not.*
>
> —Galatians 6:9 KJV

A due season or a predictable time for increase:

> *Then I will give you rain in due season, and the land shall yield her increase, and the trees of the field shall yield their fruit.*
>
> —Leviticus 26:4 KJV

A foreseeable season or specific time for blessing:

> *The LORD shall open unto thee his good treasure, the heaven to give the rain unto thy land in his season, and to bless all the work of thine hand....*
>
> —Deuteronomy 28:12 KJV

A season or an anticipated time for relief and rest:

> *And when the devil had ended all the temptation, he departed from him for a season.*
>
> —Luke 4:13 KJV

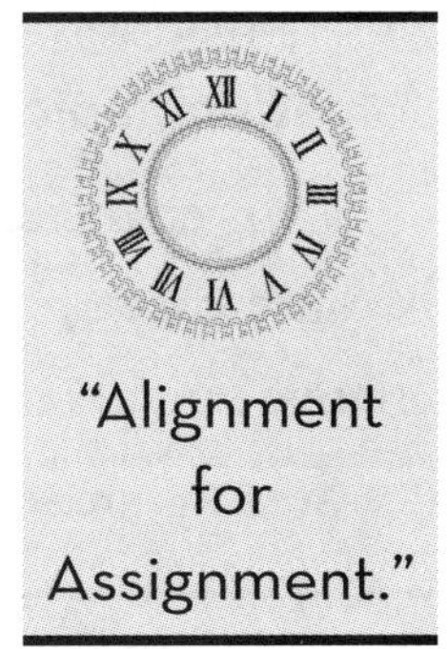

"Alignment for Assignment."

There are also seasons of attack or seasons of warfare! In Second Samuel 11:1 (NIV), it mentions *"In the spring, at the time when kings go off to war...."*

There is also a season or a specific appointed time for rest.

> *And white robes were given unto every one of them; and it was said unto them, that they should rest yet for a little season....*
>
> —Revelation 6:11 KJV

There is also what the Bible calls a season or a specific appointed time for finding miracles in specific places.

For an angel went down at a certain season into the pool, and troubled the water....

—John 5:4 KJV

A season is a clock that is meant to be read and understood. It's how things turn. The heavens and the constellations are rotational. They are a continuous prophetic circular clock. *Seasons go like clockwork and are meant to be anticipated.*

Times have to do with epic eras, small time frames defined by big events and actions.

Times Are Different from Seasons

Times are non-scheduled events defined by something epic.

Our character is very important in dealing with times because they are often unpredictable, so we have to adapt and change quickly in this kind of time.

Seasons are scheduled, so discipline is very important for our victory from season to season. We have to be able to wear two hats and partner with God both in times and in seasons.

Times are non-scheduled events defined by something epic.

Times are connected to the heart of God.

Times can be pictured in the body of Christ. In times, we are called *members* in the body of Christ. In times, you are spontaneous, fluid, relational, and everything is temporary. You are passionate and have a great since of urgency in doing your job before the fullness of time has come.

Times have to do with shifts of emphasis and our willingness to conform quickly from time to time—to gain mastery and bring our "A game" in playing our part in every new thing God has for us.

Times are connected to the heart of God.

Seasons are connected to the ways or works of God.

In seasons, we can be pictured as the temple of God. Jointly fit together in rock-solid ways. Firm and unchanging in a way that is appropriate for the narrative and theme we knew was coming and is finally here. You can count on seasons as sure as you can count on the sun coming up. When seasons get messed up, everything gets messed up.

We have to flow with God in both times and seasons. We can't do things in summer the way we do things in winter. It requires discipline. We prepare for winter in the summer because we know the next season is coming. We do not do winter in the summer time. We wait for the next season. We prepare and look for it.

To have great victory from season to season, it is imperative to go to the next level in personal revelation and insight. God shows you different sides of Him and how to love and serve Him in different times and seasons.

The Power of Twenty-Eight

Both epic linear time and circular seasonal time are classified in the one term "times and seasons" throughout the Bible. The biblical number that represents times and season is twenty-eight.

We first know this because in Ecclesiastes 3 there are 28 times and seasons listed.

Other examples of 28 line up prophetically. The phrase "ends of the earth" is in the Bible 28 times. That's interesting because those are places on the map. Acts 17:24-26 says that God has predetermined our times and places.

But Jesus will show up and bring redemption into every time and every season. That's why the term "the Lamb" and the word "cross" are found in the Bible exactly 28 times. The power of the cross is there for you in every time and in every season! Redemption for all your times.

This is why the word "courage" must be in the Bible exactly 28 times, as well. If we know that God is with us in every time and season, we can have courage and are no longer in chains of fear.

So, if we are able to identify what some of time really is, the 28 crosses and 28 lambs will bring us into what time was truly created for. That is in the next segment.

The BIG Headline from Chapter 5

There's a big difference between times and seasons. There is a supernatural, God-given ability to discern your times and seasons so you can cooperate with God.

What This Means to You

Times are more spontaneous than seasons. Times are specific eras. Seasons are predictable cycles. When you determine what season you are in, you can quickly determine what you have to accomplish in order to move into the next season. Timelines are bookended by the beginning and ending of epic events. These are easy to mark afterward. Seasons are predictable and identifiable during the appointed time, so the season following is already known.

You can be in perfect timing with both your times and your seasons so that all of God's good purposes are fulfilled in your life. Being in sync with God's timing lines you up for a powerful Kingdom advantage.

> *For He says: "In an acceptable time I have heard you, and in the day of salvation I have helped you." Behold, now is the accepted time; behold, now is the day of salvation.*
>
> —2 Corinthians 6:2

Questions to Ponder

What was an obvious timeline in my life with a beginning and an end?

Using the 28 Ecclesiastes 3 times and seasons, what time and season am I living in the following:

- My family
- My finances
- My ministry

- My job / purpose
- My walk with God

If I believe God hears and acts on my prayers for my future, do I believe He can and will answer my prayers to redeem events in my past? Why?

SECTION ONE SUMMARY

1. What We have Learned so Far

Check the box when you think you have a mental grip and peace in your heart on each point.

- ☐ Time is not God. Time is created just like you and has a beginning and an ending.
- ☐ Time is part of God's creation and is completely subject to Him. He can use time in any way and change time in any way the same way and can use and change anything He has created.
- ☐ This means He can intervene in and change your time as well.
- ☐ Time is a gift from God that progresses and blesses the redeemed, is purposeful to the redeemer, and is a curse of loss and finality for everything that is not of the Kingdom.
- ☐ Time, space, and matter are in perfect continuum. According to Genesis 1:1, God created time, space, and matter in the very beginning. If you change one, you change the other two. If God can change water into wine (matter), it is no more difficult or inappropriate for Him to change your past or your future for His redemptive purposes.

- ☐ The glory of God might best be described as "God's visible awesomeness"; and when Moses saw the backside of the glory of God, I believe He saw God's awesomeness from present/past tense. This means God can show you His goodness in your past and change everything in your now.
- ☐ When God created time, He made different kinds of time just like He made different kinds of trees, flowers, dogs, continents, planets, and even galaxies.
- ☐ There are many different kinds of time. Four new revelations of time can be called redeemed time, unredeemed time, linear time, and seasonal, or circular, time.
- ☐ Redeemed time: a flow of relative time where everything is coming, and life is progressing and being gained.
- ☐ Unredeemed time: a flow of relative time where everything is being lost, regressing, and passing away.
- ☐ Linear and cyclical timelines are also known as times and seasons.
- ☐ Times are epic prophetic eras that define things.
- ☐ Seasons are prophetic appointments defined by a narrative and a theme.
- ☐ The number 28 is a prophetic symbol for the term "times and seasons" as listed in Ecclesiastes 3.

- [ ] The word *cross* is in the Bible 28 times. This is a prophetic picture indicating there is a cross—or redemption—for every time and season in the Bible guaranteeing our victory.
- [ ] The word *Lamb* is also in the Bible 28 times, meaning there is a redemptive price that has been paid for every time and every season.
- [ ] The love of God triumphs over every form of time. He has guaranteed the redemptive power of the cross for every time and season.
- [ ] Time does not control God and doesn't have to define His people.

A Prayer of Perfect Timing

Father God, You created time and it's literally in Your hands. Make my times and my seasons praise Your holy name. Let Your goodness pass before me as I see my days, and cause me to be in perfect alignment with every Kingdom purpose in every time and season You are trusting me with.

Give me a supernatural grace and an Issachar anointing to be in perfect sync with Your heart and Your timing. I pray that I would always be at the right place, at the right time for the right miracle to happen. I love You, oh God of my past, present, and future. In Jesus' name, amen.

Lord, you know everything there is to know about me.

You perceive every movement of my heart and soul, and you understand my every thought before it even enters my mind.

You are so intimately aware of me, Lord.

You read my heart like an open book and you know all the words I'm about to speak before I even start a sentence!

You know every step I will take before my journey even begins.

You've gone into my future to prepare the way, and in kindness you follow behind me to spare me from the harm of my past.

—Psalm 139:1-5 TPT

My times are in Your hand....
—Psalm 31:15

Time is relative. When you sit with a girl for two hours it seems like two minutes. When you sit on a hot stove for two minutes it seems like two hours. That is relativity.

—Albert Einstein

Section Two

THE PURPOSE AND FUNCTION OF TIME

In this section you will learn about:

- The biblical timeline and how it works.
- Time begins at sin and ends with total redemption.
- Time is in continuum with space and matter but also with sin and death.
- The central theme of God's purpose for time.
- Hebrew timelines and Gentile timelines.
- Different perspectives of the earth's time.
- How to view your own times.
- How God can track with time.
- How that can change everything for you.
- How God can attach a redeemed history to something brand-new.

6

The Line of Time

Let's move now into the second big premise on our road to redemptive freedom.

PREMISE 2

God created time for the purpose of works of redemption.

So, God created the timeline in a way for us to actually observe it. Let's take a quick look at the biblical timeline. You will recognize it's linear, not circular, because it has a beginning and an end. It begins with the fall of Adam and ends with a new heaven and earth. Timeline example:

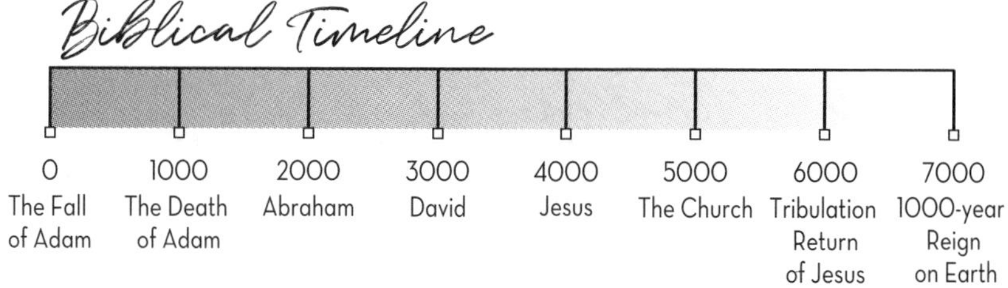

There are basically 2,000 years from Adam to Abraham, 2,000 years from Abraham to Christ, and 2,000 years from Christ to now.

That's not hard, is it? It is important you understand where the timeline begins and where it ends. If you can understand this simple truth, you can understand the meaning and the power of time.

A biblical timeline of humanity looks a like a seven-day week with every 1,000 years being a day (2 Peter 3:8). The last day, or the last one thousand years, is in the millennial reign of Jesus Christ after He comes back at the end of the Tribulation. A day of rest you might say.

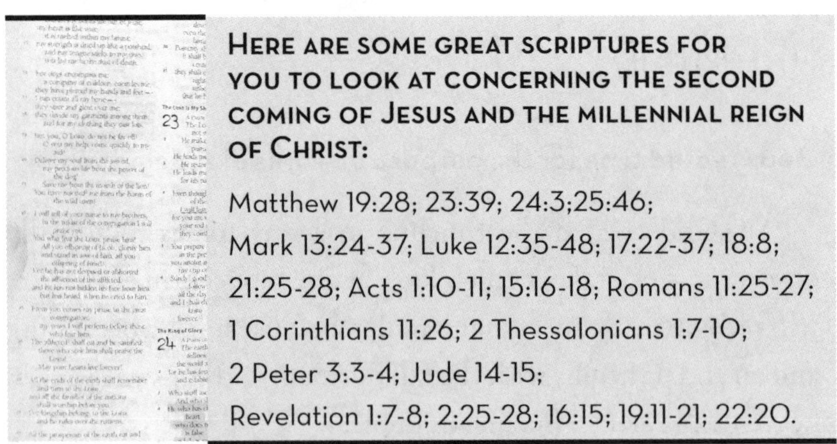

HERE ARE SOME GREAT SCRIPTURES FOR YOU TO LOOK AT CONCERNING THE SECOND COMING OF JESUS AND THE MILLENNIAL REIGN OF CHRIST:

Matthew 19:28; 23:39; 24:3;25:46;
Mark 13:24-37; Luke 12:35-48; 17:22-37; 18:8;
21:25-28; Acts 1:10-11; 15:16-18; Romans 11:25-27;
1 Corinthians 11:26; 2 Thessalonians 1:7-10;
2 Peter 3:3-4; Jude 14-15;
Revelation 1:7-8; 2:25-28; 16:15; 19:11-21; 22:20.

Go back and look at that biblical timeline.

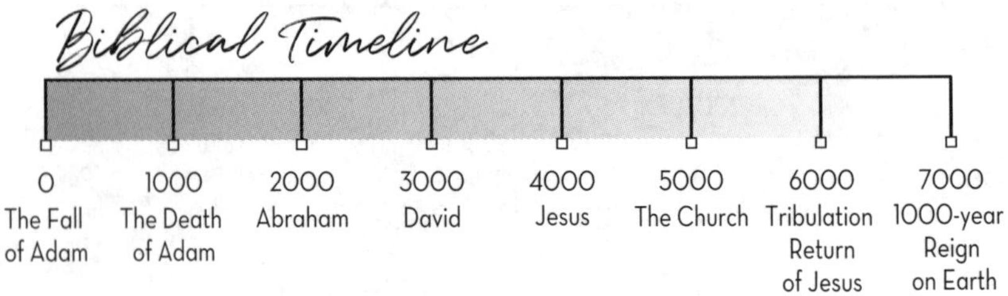

This is not a modern scientific timeline, it's a biblical one. But before we tackle those stark contrasts, this is what you get to know that the scientific world does not understand: *I believe the timeline begins at the fall of Adam and ends at the final judgment.* The reason being that time, for Adam and all of his kids, is something we have to deal with until our sin and our death has been dealt with, or judged. This actually proves the purpose God created time for. He created time and caused humankind to enter into it as soon as man entered into sin and death.

Time is not only in continuum with space and matter, time is in continuum with sin and death.

They are different, but they are inseparable so they are One.

Perfect Timing

In the last section, we reviewed the idea of continuum. Continuum is a continuous sequence in which different elements are not perceptibly different from each other. That's a fancy way of saying when things are in continuum, they are "inseparable." They may be different, but one cannot exist without the other.

I think the greatest Kingdom example of continuum might be the mystery of the Trinity—the Father, Son, and Holy Spirit. They are different, but they are inseparable so they are One.

I think Paul must have been thinking about the Hebrew version of this when he wrote his book to the Gentiles.

For I am persuaded that neither death nor life, nor angels nor principalities nor powers, nor things present nor things to come, nor height nor depth, nor any other created thing, shall be able to separate us from the love of God which is in Christ Jesus our Lord.

—Romans 8:38-39

Now that's continuum! Things that are completely different but inseparable in every way. That's going to be you, me and King Jesus for all eternity!

Getting back to time, time, space, matter, sin, and death are in perfect continuum. One cannot exist without the others. Adam had dominion over time, space, matter, sin, and death until he fell into sin. The day he fell into sin, he was subject to death, which means he was subject to time.

Why? Because it guarantees finality if there is no redemption. Time also guarantees the ability of a redemptive work to happen through the span of time. This is big. When you enter into sin and death, you automatically enter into time.

Time, space, matter, sin, and death are in perfect continuum.

Therefore, just as through one man sin entered the world, and death through sin, and thus death spread to all men, because all sinned.

—Romans 5:12

While you're traveling down the Romans Road, stop by these Scriptures as well:

But right now, the question about time is, "Why?" What was God thinking when He created it? Why would God have Adam fall into a timeline the moment he sinned, and why was he not subject to time until death was on the scene?

You see, the consequence of sin is death (time). However, *time is the only place you can find an answer or antidote for sin.* God created time for the purpose of bringing redemption.

A linear timeline with a past, present, and future is the only place Adam, or any of us, can say, "That was then, but this is now." You can't do that in eternity. So, time was designed to make sure death ruled over those who refused the gift of redemption. It was also designed as an environment to provide transformation to those who receive by this same gift.

All this means that our great Redeemer King can bring His glory and His power into any of our personal timelines and change anything by displacing what is in bondage with the Kingdom of heaven. By the way, that means if someone has power over sin, He has power over death. That also means He has power over all matter and all space for all time!

No wonder Jesus could walk through walls (dominion over matter) and show up at different places (dominion over space) once He demonstrated dominion over sin and death.

So, time for Adam began with his sin—when death entered into his life. As soon as Adam entered into sin, he entered into time. That's where the timeline begins—at the fall of Adam.

> *And the Lord God commanded the man, saying, "Of every tree of the garden you may freely eat; but of the tree of the knowledge of good and evil you shall not eat, for in the day that you eat of it you shall surely die."*
> —GENESIS 2:16-17

Adam was given dominion over everything in the garden. Time was in the garden with all other created things, but because Adam had not yet sinned, it was *redeemed time*. His dominion included redeemed time, space, and matter.

So, time for Adam began with his sin—when death entered into his life.

The moment Adam fell into sin, a trap door fell out from under him and he fell into *unredeemed time*. He stood up from the ground, everything was different, and now his clock was ticking. If Second Peter 3:8 is correct and a day is to the Lord as a thousand years, Adam dies that very same day, 930 years later (Genesis 5:5).

I don't know how long Adam lived and walked with God before he fell into the rule of the clock. Maybe a billion years, maybe one single day, I don't think anybody within our timeline knows. But I do know this: as soon as he was subject to sin and death, he was subject to the flow of unredeemed time. Adam became *subject to* time, distance, and the laws of the material world. That means he began to die and pass away.

Time's Up!

Time does not end at the death of Adam but at the end of all redemptive works for his children. It ends at the Great White Throne Judgment where sin is finally defeated and death is no more.

> *Then I saw a great white throne and Him who sat on it, from whose face the earth* [matter] *and the heaven* [space] *fled away.* ***And there was found no place for them.*** *And I saw the dead, small and great, standing before God, and books were opened. And another book was opened, which is the Book of Life. And the dead were judged according to their works, by the things which were written in the books. The sea gave up the dead who were in it, and Death and Hades delivered up the dead who were in them. And they were judged, each one according to his works. Then Death and Hades were cast into the lake of fire. This is the second death. And anyone not found written in the Book of Life was cast into the lake of fire.*
>
> —Revelation 20:11-15

Now, the very next verse says:

> *Now I saw a new heaven and a new earth, for the first heaven and the first earth had passed away....*
>
> —Revelation 21:1

When you bring an end to heaven (space) and earth (matter) you bring an end to time. Once redemption has done its work, we have no more need of time. The finality of judgment and redemption is the Great White Throne.

There is a history and future before and after death. However, it's not revealed within the timeline because it's outside of the timeline. But as it is written:

> *Eye has not seen, nor ear heard, nor have entered into the heart of man the things which God has prepared for those who love Him.*
>
> —1 Corinthians 2:9

If you are going to be skilled at bringing redemption into your past time frames, you have to understand this very important truth: *Time is the only place you can put something in your past.* Time is the only place you can have transformation from one thing to another. Once that work is completed, there is no more purpose for time, and time is finished.

Once redemption has done its work, we have no more need of time

Time was created as space for God to do redemptive works in the lives of human beings.

The BIG Headline from Chapter 6

Time for humanity begins with the fall of Adam and ends with the last chance of redemption and final act of judgment.

What This Means to You

The purpose of time is to provide a place and environment to deal with sin and death. If you still have time, you still have an opportunity to bring God's redemptive work into your life, changing things from death unto life.

If your spirit has been redeemed, your mind is being redeemed, and someday your body will be redeemed. It means time is working for you, not against you.

> *So teach us to number our days, that we may gain a heart of wisdom.*
>
> —Psalm 90:12

You should also note that since God created time for the purpose of redemptive works, it is wisdom and the proper use of time to invite God into every timeline you can think of—past, present, and future. Ask God to meet you there and do the work of His heart.

Questions to Ponder

What was my theory on the biblical timeline before reading this chapter? How has it changed after reading Pastor Troy's view of the biblical timeline?

How does the premise that the "clock started ticking" for humankind when Adam and Eve sinned change how I think of creation and the biblical timeline?

The words "a day is like a thousand years to the Lord" has long been debated. What is my current view of this verse and how it works with what I know about time.

What do I think of the statement, "God created time for the purpose of redemption"—that time is the only place we can say, "That was then. This is now"?

7

The Day the Music Died

In this short chapter, I hit the same understanding with a little different view.

The Bible clearly states that time has a beginning and an end.

That's because time is created. Time is no more a god than a sound wave or a planet. It is created so it starts and finishes. That's the biblical truth. Scientists are just now catching up with this idea. There's one theory in modern mainstream science for the origins of the universe that predicts time itself will end in just five billion short years—right around the time our sun is slated to die.

> The Bible clearly states that time has a beginning and an end.

They are correct in their theory, but they are mistaken on their dates. That's because they don't understand the beginning marker—when sin began—and the ending marker, when sin is dealt with.

You don't learn the beginning and the end unless you know the beginning and end personally. His name is Jesus.

> *I am Alpha and Omega, the Beginning and the End, the First and the Last.*
>
> —Revelation 22:13

This is how my theory works out. Let's go back to the beginning.

> *And the Lord God commanded the man, saying, "Of every tree of the garden you may freely eat; but of the tree of the knowledge of good and evil you shall not eat, for in the day that you eat of it you shall surely die."*
>
> —Genesis 2:16-17

I do not know when time began, but I think I know when time began for Adam. As already stated, Adam may have lived for billions of years, or 24 hours, before he disobeyed God and got kicked off the glorious reservation called Eden. We don't know because, outside of the seven days of creation, there is no clear reference to time. That is, until sin shows up.

Critics may scoff and say something like, "No, the Bible clearly says the evening and the morning in each day of creation marked a day so we are talking about a true 24-hour period."

I have no trouble calling the seven days of creation seven days because that's what the Bible calls it. I am not smarter than the Bible, so there is no need for me to fix it. I also do not mind pointing out that the sun was not created until the fourth day. That means the first three days had nothing to do with the consecutive period of time during which the sun is above the horizon—what you and I call a day. We also know it obviously doesn't mean the period of time during which the earth completes one rotation with respect to the sun, or a solar day. Remember, the sun hadn't been created until the fourth day.

Some might point out that Peter, as I already mentioned, says a day is like a thousand years to the Lord, and I would wholeheartedly say, "Amen" (2 Peter 3:8). But remember, a year is also the period of time the earth is moving in its orbit around the sun. So, it very well might not mean 1,000 years, 12 hours, or 24 hours because the sun wasn't created until the fourth day.

It is also extremely possible a day might mean all of those at the same time, because time is relative. We are talking about a different kind of gauge than we are now accustomed to.

> I have no trouble calling the seven days of creation seven days because that's what the Bible calls it.

Real Time

But the "day" Adam sinned turned into a very real 24-hour day as we know it now. He fell from what Sir Isaac Newton understood as absolute time (I call this redeemed time) into what Einstein describes as relative time (what I call unredeemed time). The day, or the clock, began ticking for Adam when he ate of the fruit of the knowledge of good and evil. Having lost access to the tree of life for his own protection, the laws of entropy—aka the Second Law of Thermodynamics—began to apply to him and he began to age and deteriorate. He was now dealing with the reality of unredeemed time.

Can you imagine? Adam walked with God uninhibited by the space between two distances. He wasn't ruled by the laws of gravity or the physical limitations of how his brain worked. He was more super than natural. He experienced those things but he had dominion over them just like Jesus after the resurrection. He can walk through a closed door or cover large distances in the blink of an eye. Adam was like that and someday so shall we!

Then in one horrible moment, Adam's experience changed into something different.

> *Then the eyes of both of them were opened, and they knew that they were naked; and they sewed fig leaves together and made themselves coverings.*
>
> —Genesis 3:7

His eyes, his understanding, and his worldview changed, and immediately he and his beautiful wife are trying to stitch their broken lives back together. They are now about the business of covering up shameful things.

There is no mystery to it. It's simple. However, there's a huge mystery to understanding time before Adam sinned and fell through the trap door we know as sin, which always ends in death.

> *For the wages of sin is death, but the free gift of God is eternal life in Christ Jesus our Lord.*
>
> —Romans 6:23

Sin and death are in perfect continuum. If you get rid of one, you get rid of the other. The moment Adam was contaminated with sin, he was owned by death. *Where death reigns is in matter and space. When death reigns is found in time.*

This new brutal environment meant things that shouldn't happen, happen often. Adam was introduced to anxiety, fear, and shame. Now that he was subject to the elements (matter), his body would have to fight off cancer and other illnesses. He would have to find immediate shelter. He saw his first thorn and felt his first bead of sweat. It was a different kind of bad. Nothing about dreaming here, everything about surviving for as long as you can before death finally catches you on another bad day.

Adam was fallen in every way a person could be fallen.

But nobody knew that time was God's ace up His holy sleeve to insure an environment where a redemptive work could take place. A brutal and harsh environment unlike anything in heaven but the only place where He could change somebody. The only place a promise for the future could be given or a situation changed from what is to what it should be.

So, it's there, at the very beginning of time, on the day Adam sinned, that God gives His very first promise concerning redemption by hinting at the birth of a Messiah Redeemer.

> *So the Lord God said to the serpent: "Because you have done this, you are cursed more than all cattle, and more than every beast of the field; on your belly you shall go, and you shall eat dust all the days of your life. And I will put enmity between you and the woman, and between your seed and her Seed; He shall bruise your head, and you shall bruise His heel."*
>
> —Genesis 3:14-15

The BIG Headline from Chapter 7

The clock on humanity began ticking when Adam and Eve rebelled against God and ate the fruit of the Tree of the Knowledge of Good and Evil. They fell from absolute time (redeemed) into relative time (unredeemed) where sin, age, and decay—the Second Law of Thermodynamics—leads to death.

Time is the place you fall to because death can be dealt with there, even eliminated, by redemption.

What This Means to You

You need not be afraid to invite God into your worst moments. He created time as an environment where He can enter in and actually confront the thing that is killing you—even if the death you are dealing with is self-inflicted. Because time has a past, present, and future, He can easily operate in a way that says, "From this point forward there is a future and a hope instead of a history and a dreadful outcome."

> *For I know the thoughts that I think toward you, says the Lord, thoughts of peace and not of evil, to give you a future and a hope.*
>
> —Jeremiah 29:11

Questions to Ponder

In my own words, what is the difference between absolute time and relative time?

How does this change my worldview on creation? On time itself?

Can I really consider that when I enter into sin, a certain clock begins to tick and when redemption enters in, another clock starts? What does that mean to me?

8

The History of Time

Believe me when I say the more you understand the seven days of the creation timeline and the 7,000 years of the biblical human timeline, the more you will understand your own.

Let's go deeper.

I have already discussed some of the different views of the timing of the original seven days of creation. I don't know what kind of day it was, but I know it was a good one because at the end of every day, God called it good. *I am for calling it whatever God calls it.*

The reason there is a mystery to the timing of creation is because we are dealing with sinless time. All eternity is mixed into creation in a way that we can't map out yet. It's not a linear timeline. It's a cyclical one.

Just like that, there is no clear definition of how many sunsets Adam saw or the amount of time between his birth as a full-grown man standing in the garden to the moment he was found hiding in the bushes (Genesis 3:10). After he enters into death-time, the days are well marked out, easily understandable, even predictable. Time is no longer eternal. It has now become a machine. Just like the legendary John Henry, Adam can't race long enough or fast enough against the machine of time.

The Earth's Birthday

Our Jewish brothers and sisters have a day they celebrate as the birthday of the world. On Rosh Hashanah (September 19, 2020), the first day on the Hebrew civil calendar, the Jews say the earth is 5781 years old. Our Western friends point to the year 2020 on the Gregorian calendar which is based on the death of Jesus Christ (AD). Add to this the timeline before Jesus' life, death and resurrection (BC) and the Gregorian calendar is basically saying the world is 6,021 years old.

Which one is right? Neither because we are not taking about how old the world is but how long it has been since Adam entered into sin.

Why is it when we read the Bible, it seems very clear the earth is very young and when we study science we read that the earth is very old? Why are the calendars so different?

Without a never-ending explanation, I want to throw a three-sided wrench into your gear box.

1. There is a very real anti-God bias in a big part of the scientific community that will lie, cheat, or cover up anything that points to the Creator. It's a fact that many progressive intellects and scientists worship their own understanding and have made a religion out of science—one without God in it, and they are hostile to believers.

Whatever the case, they have a much different starting point from the one given us in the Bible.

2. There is a very real anti-science bias within the worldwide Church because we think our understanding of the Bible is perfect, and it is not. We come up with ludicrous ideas like the world is flat and the universe rotates around the earth, and call it heresy when people do not believe what we believe to be true. Because most Christians are unaware of the vast amount of information on time in their Bible, they don't know where the clock begins. These people often throw the proverbial baby out with the bathwater when it comes to time.

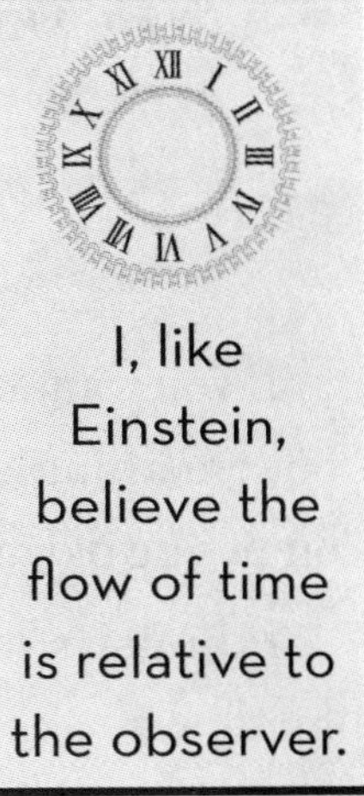
I, like Einstein, believe the flow of time is relative to the observer.

3. It may very well be that both the old earth timeline and the new earth timeline are true at the same time because time is relative.

WHAAAAAAAT?! This is where you hear the needle run across the record player and a cute little boy says, "Whatchewtalkin'bout Willis?"

Yes, one timeline is only seen by people of faith and the other by those who can only see within the timeline. I, like Einstein, believe the flow of time is relative to the observer.

I think our view of time is not only relative to speed, temperature, and mass, but to faith as well. It turns out, the condition of our heart causes us to view certain things through either a lens where you can see God, or a lens where you cannot see God. One timeline is new. The other is old.

> *By faith we understand that the worlds were framed by the word of God, so that the things which are seen were not made of things which are visible.*
>
> —Hebrews 11:3

If you want to go crazy, I can go there with you. Let me show you something else I believe is highly plausible when it comes to competing old and young earth timelines.

I think it's very possible that God actually created the earth brand-new with a built-in history. Not only to make things instantly work but to confound the wise who choose to see the design without the Designer.

Brand-New Time with a History

What if God created everything—I mean everything—in six days no matter what you want to call a day, here it comes...*with history attached to it.*

If on the seventh day, you cut down a tree that was only two days old, wouldn't it have rings in it as if it had been there for hundreds of years? Wouldn't the stones in the river already be smooth as if they had been there for thousands of years? That's not hard to imagine because God puts a great big value on maturity. How do I know? The account of the Promised Land.

> *So it shall be, when the Lord your God brings you into the land of which He swore to your fathers, to Abraham, Isaac, and Jacob, to give you large and beautiful cities which you did not build, houses full of all good things, which you did not fill, hewn-out wells which you did not dig, vineyards and olive trees which you did not plant—when you have eaten and are full.*
>
> —Deuteronomy 6:10-11

God sent the Israelites into a land that was already mature. Why? Because if they had to plow and plant, fell and build an entire society from the ground up, it would have been decades before God would be able to deal with them on the issue at hand—ridding the land of the evil nations occupying that piece of real estate God called Holy, set apart for Him and the Jewish people. God and the Jews had a relationship to rekindle and the Lord was not willing to waste any more time.

God's love of maturity is also seen in the stars. Wouldn't the light from the stars be seen on earth for times and seasons and days and years, as the Bible says, immediately on the fourth day? That means they would have a history of however many light years it would take for the light to get to our planet already attached.

> *Then God said, "Let there be lights in the firmament of the heavens to divide the day from the night; and let them be for signs and seasons, and for days and years; and let them be for lights in the firmament of the heavens to give light on the earth"; and it was so.*
>
> —Genesis 1:14-15

Firmament is a mysterious word meaning "from or for our perspective." It's what you can see from terra firma. Yet, if time-traveling Jesus stepped into the fourth day and took you with Him, you could look up and see a star called V762 with your naked eye in Cassiopeia. The conundrum is that it takes the light 16,308 years to reach the earth! This doesn't make sense unless you understand God created that star with a history of at least 16,308 years already attached to it.

That twinkling light you are looking at is already hundreds and even thousands of years old; yet in reality, it's only been there for just a few short moments on the fourth day. This also depends on which reality you are looking into—a redeemed one or an unredeemed one. Remember that our view of time is relative to many things, including our redeemed point of view or our view from the perspective of sin and death.

God's value for maturity is also seen in the first man and woman. When God breathed life into Adam as a grown man who could already stand on his very first day, wasn't his body created as if he had gone through years of growing, learning to walk, speak, and think like a grown man? Eve was a fully developed woman from the moment God created her out of Adam's rib. He did not have to push her in a baby carriage. They had to be created mature with a history of walking, talking, thinking, eating, interacting, and so on.

My theory on why carbon tests say the earth is old and the Bible says it is young is they are both accurate depending on who you put your trust in. The Creator created space and matter with a history (time). He had to because of the continuum.

Time past was created at the same time that time-present and time-future were created. He created all time at the same time.

The **BIG** Headline from Chapter 8

When you view your timeline, you either see it according to nature without a creator, which is all about history, or you view it as a creation made by our Creator and it's all about destiny.

What This Means to You

Jesus cannot only give you time now and in your future, He can create a past for you that is better than the one you have experienced. He can create that history right now.

God can create a right-now kind of time that is different from how it has been.

God can create a future that is different from how it was going to be.

God can create a history that is different from how it has been experienced because redemption changes everything. Just look at the difference between the Genesis journey of Abraham and the New Testament redeemed version of his history in Romans 4 and Hebrews 11.

God values maturity. He created Adam and Eve as fully mature with a history already attached. He didn't have to teach them to walk, talk, eat, or do the things natural humans do. Just like that, I believe all creation including trees, mountains, animals, rivers, and stars were created with a history. Trees were created with rings already in them. The light of stars could be seen from our firmament immediately from the moment God said, "Let there be..."

How you experience the reality of any timeline is relative to the lens of redemption or the lack of it.

Hold on to this truth: *When Jesus, our Messiah and Redeemer, steps into any timeline, everything changes. Not just our present and our future but even our past.*

Questions to Ponder

What did I think about the history of the world before this chapter? What do I think about it now?

Why does God value maturity?

What do I think of the theory that God created everything with a history attached to it?

If God can create a history for me right now, what are the possibilities and conclusions I can come to?

9

In Line with Time

An example of a biblical timeline:

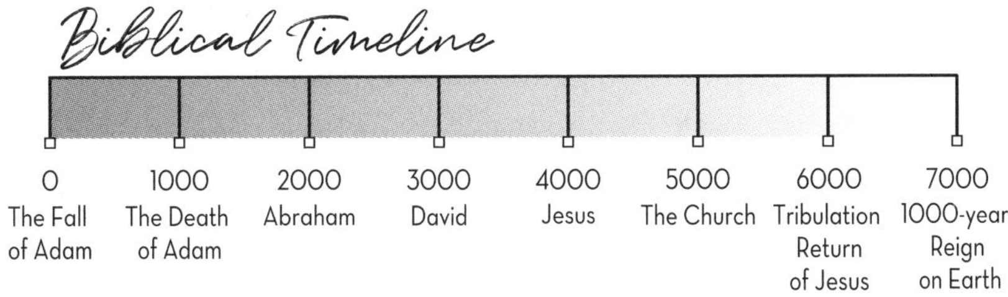

Enter the Warrior

Time is a place where Jesus can bring redemption and transformation. Jesus is not subject to time. He lives in eternity and is free to step in or out of any timeline. Let's take this a step further. Let's look at some practical, biblical precedents for this thought.

If you look at the Bible, you see a very distinct difference between the Old Testament and the New Testament:

The Old Testament ends with the words:

> *...lest I come and smite the earth with a curse.*
>
> —Malachi 4:6 KJV

The New Testament ends with:

> *The grace of our Lord Jesus Christ be with you all. Amen.*
>
> —Revelation 22:21

With Jesus, our Messiah and Redeemer, we have moved from a threat to a promise, from punishment to grace, and from a curse to a blessing. This is what happens when Jesus Christ steps into any time frame. It's what happens when time is redeemed. The Bible is divided that way, from the old to the new covenant.

Recordable time itself is also marked as before Jesus—BC, and after Jesus—AD. This is the way our lives as believers must also look. Our lives were one thing before Jesus; and after Jesus, our lives were another. Like the Bible and time itself, our life's line is divided with the game-changing marker of the entrance of Jesus Christ.

However...

A funny thing starts to happen when you find Jesus arriving in the written Word, the Bible. You start to see Him, just glimpses at first, in places you didn't see Him before. In the beginning, you see Him through typology and shadows. Then, you actually start to see Jesus in the Old Testament. You start to find Him in a history He couldn't have been in before He was made manifest.

Then after a little while longer, as you read in places like Genesis 18, Genesis 32, and Judges 13, Jesus Himself just flat out shows up thousands of years before He was born! What's He doing in this part of the timeline?

Theologians refer to the appearances of God in these passages, and others like them, as "theophanies" (Greek: *theos* = "God" + *phaino* = "appear") or "Christophanies." Therefore, these words mean "appearances of God" and "appearances of Christ," respectively, before He actually appeared in the timeline. Time travel is impossible for man, but not for Him.

Know this: There are biblical precedents for many appearances of Jesus in a timeline where Jesus doesn't actually show up until way later in that same timeline.

Jesus is the image of the invisible God (Colossians 1:15). He is at the Father's side, and He is the only One who reveals Him (John 1:18). And here are some of His pre-incarnate appearances:

1. Appearance to Abraham (Genesis 18)
2. Appearance to Jacob (Genesis 32:22-32)
3. Appearance to Joshua (Joshua 5:13-15)

Theologians also believe every visit of *"the angel of the Lord,"* or *"the angel of God,"* was a Christophany.

And this angel of the Lord must have been Jesus because He said in John 17:6, *"I have manifested your name to the* [people] *whom you gave me out of the world."*

4. Visit to Hagar (Genesis 16:7-14)
5. Visit to Abraham and Isaac (Genesis 22:11-18)
6. Visit to Jacob (Genesis 31:11-13)

The Angel of God appeared to Jacob in a dream and said, *"I am the God of Bethel, where you anointed a pillar and made a vow to me."* The God of Bethel is Yahweh (Genesis 28:13-22).

7. Visit to Moses (Exodus 3:2-6)

Jesus Christ is a time traveler; and if you have an eye to see, you can easily identify Him.

Christians generally agree these passages, and many others that mention "the Angel of the Lord," are appearances of the pre-incarnate Christ—Christ before He came in the flesh.

Here are just a few of the characteristics of this "angel" as given in the various passages:

- The "Angel" is referred to with masculine pronouns. (Genesis 16:13; Judges 6:21)
- He is identified as God. (Judges 6:11,14; Zechariah 12:8)
- He performed miracles. (Judges 6:21; 13:20)
- Gideon and Manoah thought they would die because they saw the "Angel" face to face. (Judges 6:22; 13:22)
- The "Angel" accurately foretold future events. (Judges 13:3)
- His name is "wonderful." (Judges 13:18; Isaiah 9:6)

Hey, Jesus! We see You here and it's like finding a 747 jet 3,000 years before the Wright brothers took flight. It's like finding an iPhone encased in an Egyptian tomb. I guess that's how

King David walked in the grace of God 1,000 years before grace was offered to anybody else. He found Jesus 1,000 years before Jesus was born.

Jesus Christ Is a Time Traveler

There are more biblical and practical precedents we can list to support the reality that Jesus can step in and out of any timeline. He does it, and He does it often. Just look at what the psalmist had to say in one of the most poetic and revealing passages on time in the Bible:

> *You comprehend my path and my lying down, and are acquainted with all my ways. For there is not a word on my tongue, but behold, O Lord, You know it altogether. You have hedged me behind and before, and laid Your hand upon me. Such knowledge is too wonderful for me; it is high, I cannot attain it. Where can I go from Your Spirit? Or where can I flee from Your presence? If I ascend into heaven, You are there; if I make my bed in hell, behold, You are there. If I take the wings of the morning, and dwell in the uttermost parts of the sea, even there Your hand shall lead me, and Your right hand shall hold me.*
>
> —Psalm 139:3-10

Did you see it? The psalmist knew the Creator as a time traveler not bound by space or matter. Now, read The Passion Translation and see if you understand what the writer had experienced—redemption!

> *You are so intimately aware of me, Lord. You read my heart like an open book and you know all the words I'm about to speak before I even start a sentence! You know every step I will take before my journey even begins. You've gone into the future to prepare the way, and in kindness you follow behind me to spare me from the hurt of my past. With your hand of love upon my life, you impart blessings to me. Where could I go from your Spirit? Where could I run and hide from your face? If I go up to heaven* [eternity], *you're there! If I go down to the realm of the dead* [also eternity], *you're there too! If I fly with wings into the shining dawn* [tomorrow], *you're there! If I fly into the radiant sunset* [yesterday], *you're there waiting. Wherever I go, your hand will guide me; your strength will empower me.*
>
> —Psalm 139:3-10 TPT

Jesus is in our past, our present, and our future. Nothing is hidden from Him.

> *Your eyes saw my substance, being yet unformed. And in Your book they all were written, the days fashioned for me, when as yet there were none of them.*
>
> —Psalm 139:16

> *You saw who you created me to be before I became me! Before I'd ever seen the light of day, the number of days you planned for me were already recorded in your book.*
>
> —Psalm 139:16 TPT

The ultimate Author and Finisher of our faith story (Hebrews 12:2), Jesus has been all throughout time. As a matter of fact, He likes to write the end of the book first.

> *Declaring the end from the beginning, and from ancient times things that are not yet done, saying, "My counsel shall stand, and I will do all My pleasure."*
>
> —Isaiah 46:10

Notice that the end comes before the beginning in God's economy. I believe that before He created time, space, and matter, God Almighty looked out over time to the end of the story and worked His way back to the beginning. He saw it all. Every celebration and every war. Every smile and every tear. Every wedding, baby, graduation, and funeral. He looked out over it all and said, "Let there be...."

Because the Lord knows the end of the story—your story—nothing surprises or shocks Him. He doesn't have to change His plan or have a backup. He's truly "been there done that," which should give you so much hope!

Not only is Jesus a time traveler, sometimes He takes people along for the ride.

Not only is Jesus a time traveler, sometimes He takes people along for the ride.

The most notable account of time traveling in the Bible is when Philip was transported through space and time from talking to the Ethiopian eunuch on the road south from Jerusalem to

Gaza in Acts 8:26-40. After baptizing the brother, Philip disappears and we see the Lord accessing the time-space continuum.

> *Now when they came up out of the water, the Spirit of the Lord caught Philip away, so that the eunuch saw him no more; and he went on his way rejoicing. But Philip was found at Azotus. And passing through, he preached in all the cities till he came to Caesarea.*
>
> —Acts 8:39-40

Depending on where they were on the road, we're talking a significant distance that many scholars believe to be between 34 and 50 miles. Philip traveled that in literally the blink of an eye because the Lord had another assignment for him in Azotus, which is modern-day Ashdod near Tel Aviv on the Mediterranean coast.

What would happen if Jesus Christ stepped into your life 30 years ago, right now?

The Lord also pulled John out of space and time, then planted him thousands of years in the future to see all the events recorded in the book of Revelation. Then Jesus simply put him back in the flow of the timeline He had originally pulled John out of.

Are you kidding me?

Is it possible for you and me to see Jesus in our lives before our salvation experience? Is it possible to find Jesus in our timeline before He showed up in our timeline? What would happen if Jesus Christ stepped into your life 30 years ago, right now?

If you can invite Him into your now, and if you trust Him to work all things for good in your future (Romans 8:28), you can just as easily invite Him into your past. And He is willing to go there.

The **BIG** Headline from Chapter 9

Jesus illustrates through the Bible He can travel through time and He can cause others to travel through time with Him. The Word proves He shows up and is manifest in your history as well as your destiny.

What This Means to You

As extraordinary as it is to think Jesus can step out of His eternity and into your present moment and situation, it is not any more extraordinary for you to invite Him into your past and future. He has demonstrated He is willing and able to do just that.

When Jesus creates something new in your timeline, it isn't just for right now. He brings a new history and a new future with it as well.

> *He has made everything beautiful in its time. Also, He has put eternity in their hearts, except that no one can find out the work that God does from beginning to end.*
>
> —Ecclesiastes 3:11

> *"I am the Alpha and the Omega, the Beginning and the End," says the Lord, "who is and who was and who is to come, the Almighty."*
>
> —Revelation 1:8

Questions to Ponder

Pastor Troy says Jesus is a time traveler. What examples in Scripture can I think of?

How does Psalm 139 speak to my heart about redeeming time?

Reading through the biblical accounts of Philip and John, what do I believe about the Lord's value for time travel?

10

Understanding How God Can Interact with Time

Our Myopic View of Time

We tend to have trouble with our view of time.

We have to *own* our perspective of time—take responsibility for it. We can't have a view of time that is worldly. We have to see things through the lens of the Kingdom if we are going to partner with the King. He wants us to have an amazing view of time.

He didn't create time from His point of view, rather from our own. Just like He created the heavens to be viewed from our "firmament" (Genesis 1:14-15), God created time from and for our perspective.

Remember, even science tells us that time is relative to the observer. This is an important principle in the creation of time.

We have past, present, and future time. But the past, present, and future thing is only relevant to the created things within the created timeline. God isn't bound by any of that because He is eternal and lives in eternity where there is no time.

Not only is my past not His, it's also not yours. I mean my past is only my past and your past is only your past. It doesn't belong to anybody else. Time is relative to the observer. Time is personal and relative to the one who is experiencing time. Though our timelines may cross, they are not the same. This is really important to understanding how heaven can invade your life.

God does not have past, present, or future. He made that crystal clear when He appeared to Moses in the form of a burning bush and said these immortal words:

> *"I AM That I AM."*
>
> —Exodus 3:14 KJV

No apologies, no excuses or explanations. God says, "I just Am." He had no beginning and He has no end. He just is and He has always been, which is a picture of eternity. Daniel understood this when he called the Lord "Ancient of Days." That's the intellectual way to say, "Older than Time."

God can clearly see our perspective within our own timeline and work with us accordingly. He doesn't mind at all dealing with our perspective because He can see it all. He's the Alpha and Omega, Beginning and the End (Revelation 22:13).

Jesus is the One Who Is and Was and Is to Come (Revelation 1:8), all at the same time.

Jesus is also the same yesterday, today, and forever (Hebrews 13:8), all at the same time.

God showed me how to look at time, and I want to share it with you. Let's start off by looking at another brother's personal revelation of time.

People who study time, not mere mortals like you and I, but scientists, physicists, and people with giant 50-pound heads study Albert Einstein. The world-famous German-Jew, Einstein was an amazing thinker under all that wild hair. If you look up the word *genius,* his picture is probably right there beside the definition.

Inevitably, those who study Einstein and his life will learn of a giant cuckoo clock in Bern, Switzerland. God used this clock to mess with Einstein's brilliant mind and bring a profound revelation of how time works. It's the equivalent of the Newton's apple moment, but this one comes with a gong and dancing bears.

The Day Time Changed

Surrounded by mountains, Bern, Switzerland, is a beautiful city with a majestic river bending through it. This clock sits in the middle of amazing medieval architecture, sounds off in three tones, and features dancing bears and a crested rooster at the top of the hour.

One day in 1905 while on a street car, Einstein quit thinking about his wife, Mileva, and his love affair with "Lina," his cherished violin. As his street car moved farther away from the clock, he had a supernatural epiphany that would change the world's view of the universe.

Suddenly, Einstein understood that if light was coming from a moving train it would appear faster to somebody outside of the train than to the person sitting on the train. Even though the speed of light never changes.

If you're on the train and shining a light from the front, the speed of light would be 386,000 miles per second. But if the train was moving at 30 miles an hour, the guy outside the train could clock the speed of light as 386,030 miles per second.

Einstein's brain began to understand that even time itself would be different for the person inside the fast-moving train than for the person sitting at the clock in the middle of town. It all had to do with the view of the observer whether moving or stationary. Time, space, and the speed of time was relative to the observer.

Today, Einstein's Theory of Special Relativity is the cornerstone of our understanding of how time and matter relate to each other.

Now, I don't know much about all of that, but I had my own thunderstruck revelation on how time works, and I need to explain it to you.

From Time to Time

About 90 years later, I was sitting in my truck on Farm Road 917 in Joshua, Texas, waiting for a train to pass.

Joshua, unlike Switzerland, is flat and not very pretty. There's no beautiful river running through it. However, there is something you can see at least three times every hour and it's quite an event. A seemingly never-ending, all day line-up of 100-plus, graffiti-covered box cars and coal trains. It's miserable because every train takes at least ten minutes and typically another train is waiting.

Joshua is the highest point in Johnson County, so the big engines move extremely slow before picking up speed and allowing traffic to get by.

It was a summer day and, once again, I was the victim of the old Trinity and Brazos Valley Railway. I was watching these cars pass in front of me very slowly, one at a time.

At about train car number 40, I looked down the track and couldn't tell how long the train was. I wished I had a drone or a helicopter to get an aerial view of the entire length of the train. In my 10-pound head, I began to visualize what the train looked like from way above. I didn't have anything else to do.

EUREKA! As I imagined this view from above, I instantly had a crazy cool revelation and knew God was speaking to me. What I am about to share with you is the third premise and most important key to a revelation that will change your life for all time.

Let's look at this train as if it is our timeline of life.

From my perspective of time, I can see only one moment at a time—like my perspective of each passing train car. It goes by slowly and is only a tiny fragment of the length of the entire train. However, from God's perspective, 1,000 feet up, He can see the beginning, the middle, and the end of my timeline *all at the same time* (Isaiah 46:10).

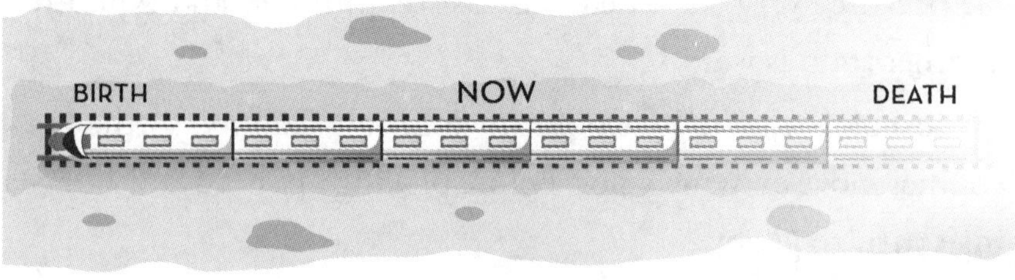

My view of time is so myopic, or nearsighted, I can only perceive the moment, or the part of the train, I am walking in right now. But God's view of time is not limited because He is not subject to time at all. He's not just on the train. He is actually above it all. He can see the beginning and the end, *right now.*

At the time you are reading this, your experience is limited to the right now. That's the confine of your place on the train or in your life's timeline.

But God sees you in your entire timeline. He sees where you have been, where you are, and where you are going to be *all at the same time.* He is right now watching you be born and watching you take your last breath of earth's air.

God can see the part of the train where you are learning to walk and your first day of school. He passes the part of your timeline where you are now, and looks into the part of the train where something amazing is happening in your distant future. Personal timeline example:

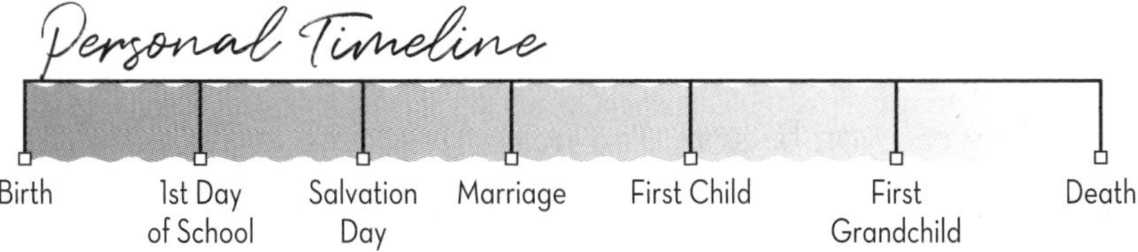

God can also step in and out of your timeline any place He wants to, the same as He can step onto the train at any car He wants to.

Right now, He can be with you at the moment of your birth or even while you were being formed—like He did with Jeremiah.

> *...I knew you before you were born....*
>
> —Jeremiah 1:5

Right now, God can be with you in your last few moments of life and make sure your death will glorify Him. He did this with Peter in John 21:19 when Jesus told him *"by what death he would glorify God."* In essence, Jesus told Peter, "I've seen your finish. I know how this story goes. I know how your death is going to glorify me, Peter." All the while, He is with you right now.

Just like that, Paul says those who are saved are already counted among the citizens of heaven and "seated in heavenly places."

> *Even when we were dead in trespasses, made us alive together with Christ (by grace you have been saved), and raised us up together, and made us sit together in the heavenly places in Christ Jesus.*
>
> —Ephesians 2:5-6

How can you be seated in heavenly places at the same time as you are reading this chapter? Because in God's view of your life, He sees it all at the same time. Like Peter, He's telling you, "I see you today, but I also see your end and it glorifies Me. You did it! You made it, so keep going."

This revelation has serious ramifications of what it means for our right now and the reality of how we experience time.

Stop a second and let it sink in.

Before your brain starts smoking, let's rehash some basic steps into this mind-blowing revelation and keep it fresh.

1. Time is God's way of keeping everything from happening at once. He is the God of order. He wants certain things worked out and accomplished.
2. Time is created by God for the purpose of redemption.
3. God is not subject to time or confined by it in any way. He is eternal and rules both time and

eternity. He can step into or pull out of any time or place He pleases.

4. God is with us now in our time frame. He is also with us in our past, in our future, and—this next part is very important—***NOW.***

No Big Deal. You've Got This!

So, here it comes. This is where it starts to get really fun.

I am not saying you can go back into your past because you can't, unless the Lord takes you there Himself. I am saying that you can invite Jesus to bring you a redeemed past that is different from what you have experienced. I am also saying that you can invite Jesus into your past because He can and does go there. If Jesus shows up in specific moments of time in your past and applies His blood, it will instantly change your "right now." This is the power of the redemptive work of Jesus.

> We have just wrongly believed that God is subject to our flow of time. He is not.

I believe this is the reason God created time in the first place. He wanted to step into our timeline, apply redemption, and transform us for the future.

We already believe that. We have just wrongly believed that God is subject to our flow of time. He is not.

Right now is the future of our past. If I am cursed right now because of something that happened in my past, I can ask Jesus—right now—to step into that moment in time, and rule and reign. That would certainly change how that moment affects me in the flow of time I am currently in. It would also change the course of my future.

Our God actually time travels at His own discretion and leisure.

When Jesus shows up in my past to redeem something there, my right now begins to change because that part of my timeline has been redeemed. The curse no longer produces from that place, and now His glory is filling my life from that place.

Enter the Redeemer

Because of this, *you and I do not have to be caged by our past.* We can't go back through time unless the One who orders time takes us there. However, as born-again believers, we are in relationship with Someone who can go back.

You will learn in the next section that relationship causes God to change the timing of things for the purposes of redemption. Our God actually time travels at His own discretion and leisure.

When the Messiah Redeemer applies His blood to that moment, everything after that changes from a curse into a blessing—from something that produces death into something that produces life.

It's not too late to invite Jesus into a past events that are causing you pain and torment today. Time is relevant. One of the things that changes how time acts is when it comes into contact with redemption. Redemption changes time. The blood of Jesus is the matter that changes time and space.

Redemption changes everything. Our time-traveling Savior cannot only bring transformation to our future, He can change our right now, because right now, we are living in yesterday's future.

> *And for this cause he is the mediator of the new testament, that by means of death, for the redemption of the transgressions that were under the first testament, they which are called might receive the promise of eternal inheritance.*
>
> —Hebrews 9:15 KJV

The blood of Jesus is the matter that changes time and space.

The **BIG** Headline from Chapter 10

God sees and is interacting with your past and your future right now. He knows you in your entire timeline, all of it, right now.

What This Means to You

You do not have to be caged or shackled by your past, no matter how terrible the events you have experienced. Nothing is wasted in the Kingdom and when His Kingdom comes into your timeline, King Jesus brings more than your present life with Him. He also brings a history and a future with Him!

He literally changes a death-producing event into a life-producing event when He is made manifest in that event. When He says He makes all things new (Revelation 21:5), He is not just being poetic. All things in your timeline can be made new and produce the newness of life and life more abundantly.

> *Therefore we were buried with Him through baptism into death, that just as Christ was raised from the dead by the glory of the Father, even so we also should walk in newness of life.*
>
> —Romans 6:4

Questions to Ponder

After reading these chapters, how has my view of the biblical timeline changed? Why?

How do eternity and time differ? How does God work in time that He doesn't work in eternity?

Are there times in my life where I can look back and see where God has moved me into a place of maturity—a place I didn't have to start from scratch? Why do I think God did this?

How would I describe eternity and time to a friend now that I've had a new revelation of time, space, and matter from Genesis 1:1?

Do I trust that God not only sees my beginning (engine) and my end (caboose) from His place in eternity, but that He can and will enter any frame of time (boxcar) within my timeline (entire train) to redeem that time by His blood? Why?

And this brings us to the section of this book on redemption.

SECTION TWO SUMMARY

What We have Learned so Far

Check the box when you think you have a mental grip and peace in your heart on each point.

- ☐ In the biblical timeline, there are basically 2,000 years from Adam to Abraham, 2,000 years from Abraham to Christ, and 2,000 years from Christ until now.
- ☐ The timeline begins at the fall of Adam and ends at the final judgment.
- ☐ Adam was not subject to time until he sinned, because he was not subject to death until he sinned.
- ☐ The moment Adam sinned, a trap door fell out from under him, he fell from something eternal into a flow of time that has a beginning and an end, and he began to die.
- ☐ Sin is in continuum with death.
- ☐ Sin, death, time, space, and matter are all in continuum. If you enter into sin, you enter into death. If you enter into death, you enter into time and are owned by time, distance (space) and the elements (matter).
- ☐ Now, this is really bad news unless there is an answer to the problem of sin and death problem. If you could get rid of sin, you could get rid of

death. The chain that would follow would be time, space, and matter would no longer dominate you.

- ☐ The consequence of sin is death (time). However, time is the only place you can bring the answer to sin.
- ☐ God created time for the purpose of bringing redemption.
- ☐ A linear timeline with a past, present, and future is the only place Adam, or any of us, can say, "That was then, but this is now." You can't do that in eternity.
- ☐ You are not shackled to the flow of time because you are in relationship with King Jesus. He is the Creator and Wielder of time.
- ☐ Jesus illustrates throughout the Bible that He can create past time, as well as present, and future time.
- ☐ Jesus illustrates throughout the Bible that He is present both before and after His own timeline on earth.
- ☐ Jesus can create something new with a redeemed history attached to it.
- ☐ The way you see time is relative to your relationship with Jesus and your heart's position of faith.
- ☐ The way you can see the beginning and end of a train as if you are suspended above the train, is something like the way God can view time. He

sees Adam's fall, Abraham's faith, David's slaying of Goliath at the same time He is seeing you read this book. He is also seeing the rapture of the Church and the return of King Jesus. Again, this is right now and all at the same time.

- ☐ Furthermore, He can step onto the train anywhere He pleases and interact with the passengers however He wants.
- ☐ God can see your personal timeline all at once. He can see your conception, your birth, your wedding day, your middle age, old age and death simultaneously—right now.
- ☐ Because we can invite Him to step into our now to change our future, we can just as easily invite Him into our past to change our now.

A Prayer for God to Invade Our Times with Heaven's Eternity

Father God, You are welcome in all my times. I pray in the name of King Jesus that Your Kingdom will come into all my days and years, past, present, and future.

Where things have been halted, I pray for accelerated time frames. Let what should take years happen in just a moment so I can get into better places. Lord, let my learning and understanding be as though I have a history, as You did with the first man, Adam. I pray that You would speed up and slow down my experience of time to benefit my experience with You. I pray that any place in my past where I have missed my calling and purpose, You would visit me in that place and be King in my life. Work all things out for my good. I repent of any time I have run or hid from You, and ask that You make Your visible awesomeness manifest in that day and in that hour. I pray, King Jesus, that You would inhabit my future in glorious places. Invite and call me there, Lord. Lead and even change my steps in my now to cause me to meet You in my future.

Your creation is beautiful, Lord. Establish Your throne in all my house, all my family, all my life, and all my time. In Jesus' name. Amen.

When it comes to time, the two most important days in your life are the day you are born and the day you find out why.

—Mark Twain

PREMISE 3

Redemption Changes Everything

In this section you will learn about:

- What redemption is and how it works
- What redemption changes and transforms
- The exchanging power of redemption
- How redemption interacts with time
- How God changes the timing of things influenced by relationship
- How redemption changes the order of things
- How redemption changes time, space, and matter
- The benefits of redemption
- How we access redemption through faith

Section Three

THE REDEEMER AND THE POWER OF REDEMPTION

If you are going to practice redeeming time and if you are going to glorify the Lord, you need to have next-level understanding of what redemption is, how it works, and what it does. Allow yourself to learn and appreciate redemption the way you would if someone gave you a giant mansion. Explore and celebrate redemption. This section will help you do that.

11

The Price Has Been Paid

It's the central theme of the entire Bible. It's the prophetic story the heavens declare to the glory of God. It's what Jesus Christ came to bring and who He Himself became—*redemption.*

> Redemption is the act of buying something back or paying a price or ransom to return something to your possession. Redemption is the English translation of the Greek word *agorazo,* meaning "to purchase in the marketplace." In ancient times, it often referred to the act of buying a slave. It carried the meaning of freeing someone from chains, prison, or slavery.
>
> —Jack Zavada, ThoughtCo.com

Redemption changes everything. Not just over time but for *all* time.

Redemption changes everything. Not just over time but for *all* time.

As far as the east is from the west, so far has He removed our transgressions from us.

—Psalm 103:12

Time and space (distance) are in perfect continuum. When God says He has removed our transgression from all distance, east to west, He is also saying redemption overcomes all time, from the beginning to the end. From our firmament or perspective, the north and south have ending points, the poles. But the east and the west do not.

Why would the Lord specifically remove our sins and throw them as far as the east is from the west—a picture of eternal separation? Because He wants them removed completely so we cannot pick them back up again. When Jesus removes them, He removes them for all time and space.

There is nothing created that redemption doesn't change. Redemption is what happens when Jesus steps onto any scene and has His amazing way. It's what He brings every time to everything in time.

When redemption changes the time, *redemption changes everything within that time from a curse to a blessing.*

Redemption also changes lost people to family, hated people to celebrated, and wicked people to holy. Redemption changes leprous bodies to perfect human specimens. Redemption brings enslaved people into freedom and transforms dead things into living things.

Through the transformational power of redemption, messed up minds become gifted learners, and shameful and pitiful people become honored and confident. I cannot tell you how much I love redemption.

Redemption changes ownership; and when things move from the Kingdom of hell to the Kingdom of heaven, the King of kings gets to have His glorious dominion and His will on earth as it is in heaven.

Redemption is beautiful because our Redeemer is beautiful.

The power of redemption is an awesome resource God brings to the table. The power to buy back those of us who are enslaved isn't bought with money. *Redemption is when Jesus brings Jesus to the table.*

Only Jesus can redeem us.

> *Those who trust in their wealth and boast in the multitude of their riches, none of them can by any means redeem his brother, nor give to God a ransom for him—for the redemption of their souls is costly, and it shall cease forever—that he should continue to live eternally, and not see the Pit.*
>
> —Psalm 49:6-9

Redemption is the single most wonderful and precious "thing" inside or outside of the created universe. Why? Because it is the spotless and pure *life* of Jesus Christ. His blood is the matter the changes time and space.

The blood is the life (Leviticus 17:11). His blood is the essence of His life and it was spent and poured out to pay the terrible price for our filth so we would no longer be slaves to sin.

> *Knowing that you were not redeemed with corruptible things, like silver or gold, from your aimless conduct received by tradition from your fathers, but with the precious blood of Christ, as of a lamb without blemish and without spot.*
>
> —1 PETER 1:18-19

The Jews understand that the blood of an unblemished lamb makes them like that lamb—spotless. This is why the prophet Isaiah said the following:

> *"Come now, and let us reason together," says the Lord, "Though your sins are like scarlet, they shall be as white as snow; though they are red like crimson, they shall be as wool."*
>
> —ISAIAH 1:18

In the Jewish culture, this is a picture of taking a red piece of cloth and un-dyeing it. The only way to do this is by turning back the clock and redeeming time. While in the natural this is impossible, in the supernatural that's what the sacrificial lamb did for them. It turned back time, and that's what the blood of Jesus does for all who believe.

The Redeemer Brings It

At His very first sermon, Jesus proves this point as He quotes Isaiah and delivers His mission statement of bringing redemption.

> *The Spirit of the Lord is upon me, because he hath anointed me to preach the gospel to the poor; he hath sent me to heal the brokenhearted, to preach*

> *deliverance to the captives, and recovering of sight to the blind, to set at liberty them that are bruised.*
>
> —Luke 4:18 KJV

Now when the Spirit of the Lord is upon you, that is different from being with you or in you. The Spirit "upon" you is an anointing for a specific action to accomplish something amazing.

What was Christ, which means "anointed One," anointed to do?

1. Reach the poor—people who had never been granted access—with redemption.
2. Heal the brokenhearted—bring hope and love of life to people who had been broken—with redemption.
3. Set captives free by redemption.
4. Restore sight and understanding to the blind by redemption.
5. Set people free from what beat them up; *"to set at liberty them that are bruised."* Bruised is when you are beat up on the inside, and wounded is when you are beat up on the outside. All this by paying a price only He could pay.

The New Bible Dictionary defines redemption: "Redemption means deliverance from some evil by payment of a price." Now think about that amazing definition for a bit: "deliverance from some evil by payment of some price." It's all about confronting the things that own us.

Buying Slaves

I run an organization called Answer International that rescues girls and boys from sex trafficking worldwide. Since November 2016, we have had the privilege of redeeming 3,126 girls from sex slavery and restoring them to a life of freedom and hope.

I know something firsthand about the power of redemption. I have gone into brothels and rescued little girls. I took them by the hand and delivered them to a home where they are protected and allowed to be happy. Jesus restored what was stolen from them and they are now blessed to live the life of redeemed little girls—not the sex slaves of selfish monsters.

My teams work tirelessly in Southeast Asia, Nepal, India, Africa, Belize, and Nicaragua. They are bringing the power of redemption in the most tangible way I can imagine—through literally setting slaves free and restoring them to an identity and purpose of freedom.

This is what redemption does. After redemption makes its transaction, freedom, transformation, and renewal will follow.

Take another biblical look at what redemption brings so you can learn to walk in the gifts the Redeemer has given you.

The Exchange of Redemption

If redemption declares we are not guilty, that means none of the penalties of sin or lawlessness are allowed to chain us or enslave us. No shame, guilt, or feeling the horrible dishonor of deserved judgment belongs to us once redemption comes.

> *Christ's redemption has freed us from guilt. Justified freely by His grace through the redemption that is in Christ Jesus.*
>
> —ROMANS 3:24

At the same time, another declaration is proclaimed. Redemption also declares we are *worthy* of the gifts, rewards, and benefits of being holy.

The benefits of redemption include:

- Eternal life (Revelation 5:9-10)
- Forgiveness of sins (Ephesians 1:7)
- Righteousness (Romans 5:17)
- Freedom from the law's curse (Galatians 3:13)
- Freedom from guilt and shame (Romans 3:24)
- Freedom from accusation (John 8:11)
- Complete justification (Romans 3:24)
- Adoption into God's family (Galatians 4:5)
- Deliverance from sin's bondage (Titus 2:14; 1 Peter 1:14-18)
- Peace with God (Colossians 1:18-20)
- The in-dwelling of the Holy Spirit (1 Corinthians 6:19-20)

To be redeemed, then, is to be forgiven, holy, justified, free, adopted, and reconciled. See also Psalm 130:7-8; Luke 2:38; and Acts 20:28.

You have to make a big deal out of redemption. Before we get into how redemption changes time, take a moment to consider how redemption changes you.

If you are going to have a true revelation of God's heart toward you, you must have a true revelation of God's gift and acts of redemption toward you.

> *Bless the Lord, O my soul, and forget not all His benefits.*
>
> —Psalm 103:2

The BIG Headline from Chapter 11

Redemption is the ultimate game-changer. Redemption is God's plan for transforming all created things. Redemption is what Jesus brings when invited into a place and His presence changes everything.

What This Means to You

If you can believe in the power of redemption, you can believe in the power of transformation. The very act of redemption is like the un-dyeing of a red cloth—while impossible in the natural, it is possible in the supernatural because Jesus paid that price in time for all eternity.

Questions to Ponder

What has been my view of redemption in the past?

What is my view of redemption now?

How does relationship play into redeeming time?

How does the un-dyeing of a red cloth give the example of redeeming time through the blood of Jesus?

12

Redeeming Time and Matter

Redemption is eternal and time cannot limit the power of redemption. Redemption is higher than everything within the timeline because it doesn't come from time. It comes from heaven—eternity. When redemption enters time, it trumps time in every way.

> *By that will we have been sanctified through the offering of the body of Jesus Christ once for all. And every priest stands ministering daily and offering repeatedly the same sacrifices, which can never take away sins. But this Man* [Jesus Christ], *after He had offered one sacrifice for sins forever, sat down at the right hand of God,*
>
> —Hebrews 10:10-12
> (see Hebrews 10:5-9 for context)

The redemption of Jesus Christ dealt with the problem of sin *"once for all."* All means all; past, present, and future. His sacrifice for sins was *one* by which He obtained "eternal redemption" (Hebrews 9:12). That's why there is now no need for other sacrifices as Hebrews 10:18 very plainly tells us:

> *Now where there is remission of these, there is no longer an offering for sin.*

When redemption is applied to your life in your timeline, redemption interrupts and changes how the rules work in time.

The blood of Jesus is applied to past, present, and future sin of the person being redeemed. It is one redemption for all time for all sin.

> [Jesus] *gave himself for us, that He might redeem us from all iniquity....*
>
> —TITUS 2:14 KJV

Jesus Christ redeemed us "from all iniquity," and He obtained it by giving Himself for us. In other words, He was the ransom of our redemption from "all iniquity" and as already stated for all time. This is important to understand when it comes to redeeming time.

When eternal redemption enters into time and space, the very history of time is changed. When the blood is applied, sins are forgotten, and there is no more need—ever—for another sacrifice because the sin is eliminated for all time. It changes what is in the flow of time.

As a matter of fact, redemption changes matter.

A closer look shows us not just spiritual things, but literal physical properties change when the blood of Jesus Christ is applied. Time, space, and matter are subject to the dominion that redemption brings.

Let's look closely at Matthew's account of how Jesus brought redemption into physical matter. In this case, the body of a brother who couldn't move his body.

> *So He got into a boat, crossed over, and came to His own city. Then behold, they brought to Him a paralytic lying on a bed. When Jesus saw their faith, He said to the paralytic, "Son, be of good cheer; your sins are forgiven you."*
>
> —Matthew 9:1-2

By faith, they gained access to the forgiveness of sins. Redemption changes a sinner into a saint. Jesus has entered into the picture and now all is forgiven. This is going to be a problem with the onlooking religious people.

> *And at once some of the scribes said within themselves, "This Man blasphemes!" But Jesus, knowing their thoughts, said, "Why do you think evil in your hearts? For which is easier, to say, 'Your sins are forgiven you,' or to say, 'Arise and walk'?"*
>
> —Matthew 9:3-5

Jesus is saying they are both the same. The same power to forgive (change time) is the same power to heal (change matter).

> *"But that you may know that the Son of Man has power on earth to forgive sins"—then He said to the paralytic, "Arise, take up your bed, and go to your house." And he arose and departed to his house. Now*

> *when the multitudes saw it, they marveled and glorified God, who had given such power to men.*
>
> —Matthew 9:6-8

Did you catch it? The authority and power to change time, space, and matter all comes from redemption because they are all in continuum. If your sins can be forgiven, and they can, then your physical body can also be healed. The muscles can grow, the nerves can connect, and suddenly you are dancing instead of being carried.

In order for a healing to happen, matter must be supernaturally transformed. Well, isn't that what the blood of Jesus has done—supernaturally transformed us? Is not the blood of Jesus actually supernatural matter? The same redemption power that changes you from spiritually dead to spiritually living can also enter into matter and change water into wine or creatively grow muscles and strength in a guy who was paralyzed.

Jesus might have well as said, "Which is easier, to forgive sins or change the physical properties of matter?" *All of the physical miracles recorded in the Bible are the result of redemption changing matter.*

Miracles in the Bible are sometimes called signs, wonders, or even "mighty deeds." Out of the unknown number of miracles Jesus performed before His resurrection, the Bible mentions 36; all of them have to do with redemption entering into matter.

When Jesus stopped the storm and walked on water, He had to literally overrule the laws of physics. I am telling you this is what redemption has the capacity and authority to do. When Jesus multiplies the two little loaves of bread and three fishes into enough food to feed more than 5,000 hungry people, matter had to be changed, created, and multiplied.

Even today, if you have been healed of cancer or a back problem, the redemptive power of Jesus Christ has had dominion over the matter of your physical body. It's is by the supernatural blood from His back, or by His stripes, you were healed.

> *Who Himself bore our sins in His own body on the tree, that we, having died to sins, might live for righteousness—by whose stripes you were healed.*
>
> —1 Peter 2:24

Jesus took a physical beating to gain the right as a man to change physical matter.

So, redemption forgives sins and changes matter. And we know that time, space, and matter are one in perfect continuum so redemption also changes time and space.

It is real when Jesus says, *"All authority has been given to Me in heaven and on earth"* (Matthew 28:18).

Now, here is the showstopper.

Because Jesus has shown us through the centuries that He can bring the power of redemption into our physical bodies (matter), why would we not think it possible to bring Him into our timelines? If you can bring redemption in to change matter, you can also bring it in to time and space. You can redeem your time the same way you can redeem your physical circumstances.

Things get really good from here.

The BIG Headline from Chapter 12

Redemption (forgiveness of sins) trumps time, space, and matter. It gives Jesus the authority to overrule them and change the entire continuum.

It is just as easy for Jesus to change the properties of time as it is to change the physical properties of matter. Healing is a good example.

What This Means to You

It's demonstrated. It's real. It's not weird or outrageous to act upon the reality of Jesus changing time, space, and physical properties to His glory through redemption. It's normal in the Kingdom.

Get it settled. This is for you.

Questions to Ponder

How does forgiveness relate to time?

How does healing relate to matter?

How does faith work in the act of redeeming time?

How does forgiveness of sin change time and matter?

Do I have the faith to believe God would change time, space, and even matter to redeem sickness in my physical body? A painful event from my past that is affecting my today?

13

When Redemption Changes Timing and Adds Time for the Sake of Relationship

Since we are talking about Jesus changing matter through redemption, let's take a moment and actually read John's account of the miracle of water turned to wine.

> *On the third day there was a wedding in Cana of Galilee, and the mother of Jesus was there. Now both Jesus and His disciples were invited to the wedding. And when they ran out of wine, the mother of Jesus said to Him, "They have no wine."*
>
> —John 2:1-3

This miracle starts off with the time stamp of "the third day." Things rise up on the third day and redemption reigns on the third. The land rose up out of the water on the third day of creation and Jesus Himself rose from the tomb on the third day after Passover.

Now Mary, the mother of Jesus, comes and tells Him this poor young couple had run out of wine and that's a shameful thing at a Jewish wedding party.

The response of Jesus to His mother is another reference to time. He tells her that the timing is off for redemption to enter into this mess of humanity.

> *Jesus said to her, "Woman, what does your concern have to do with Me? My hour has not yet come." His mother said to the servants, "Whatever He says to you, do it."*
>
> —John 2:4-5

Trusting more in relationship with Him than in the hour, Jesus' mother turns and gives her last biblically recorded words. She says in essence, "Get ready to act upon His word." Get ready to do something because things are about to change.

Mary knew that everything in the Kingdom is relational before it is functional, and her relationship with Jesus was very special. The moment didn't define anything but her relationship with Him. Time is relevant to our relationship with Jesus.

Changing the Moment of Time

Now, this is not the first time Mary's influential relationship compelled Jesus to change His timing for the purpose of that relationship.

Twenty-one years earlier when Jesus was only twelve, Mary and Joseph lost Jesus in the hustle and the bustle of the Passover caravan. Again, we find the time stamp of the third day and watch what happens.

> *Now so it was that after three days they found Him in the temple, sitting in the midst of the teachers, both listening to them and asking them questions. And all who heard Him were astonished at His understanding and answers. So when they saw Him, they were amazed; and His mother said to Him, "Son, why have You done this to us? Look, Your father and I have sought You anxiously."*
>
> *And He said to them, "Why did you seek Me? Did you not know that I must be about My Father's business?" But they did not understand the statement which He spoke to them.*
>
> *Then He went down with them and came to Nazareth, and was subject to them, but His mother kept all these things in her heart. And Jesus increased in wisdom and stature, and in favor with God and men.*
>
> —Luke 2:46-52

Jesus changed the time from Him being in authority to becoming subject to them. It was His relationship with Mary that caused Him to change the timing of His ministry. Once He wanted to start earlier and another He wanted to start later. Mary never forgot this precedent. The Bible said she "kept them in her heart" and "pondered these things." Once again, she pulled out her special relationship card to change His timing.

Getting back to the when Jesus changed the timing of when He would start doing miracles, the Bible says His miracle also reversed the order of timing of how things normally work.

> *When the master of the feast had tasted the water that was made wine, and did not know where it came from (but the servants who had drawn the water knew), the master of the feast called the bridegroom. And he said to him, "Every man at the beginning sets out the good wine, and when the guests have well drunk, then the inferior. You have kept the good wine until now!"*
>
> —John 2:9-10

When Jesus changes the timing of things, He does it for the sake of relationship, and it changes the natural order of timing into a redeemed state. These miracles of redemption are always for the benefit of those in relationship with Him.

Jesus changed the timeline of Lazarus and added years to his life because of relationship. He literally pulled him out of death and stood him up in bad need of a bath.

Do you realize Jesus will change the timing of things for you because He loves you? Did you know, like Mary, you can ask Jesus to start something earlier or put something off until later?

Did you know that when Jesus brings redemption into the common messes of humanity, He tends to change the timing of how it usually goes? He will even reverse the way things "always" happen.

"Well, you're old, so it's probably time for you to get sick," the devil will tell you. Not if redemption comes in. Your healthiest years could be your last years.

"You're young, so it will be years and years before you are able to become successful," the devil might mumble. Not if redemption changes your time frame.

When Jesus changes something in time, He can also change the timing itself. Redemption can accelerate your time and cause things that should take a year to happen in day. Redemption can cause the things that should have happened at the first to actually happen in the end. Redemption can switch the timing from inactivity to miracles being manifest.

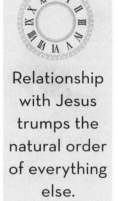

Relationship with Jesus trumps the natural order of everything else.

In the classic story of redemption found in the book of Ruth, the mother-in-law of our heroine experienced this shift in redemptive timing. As an old woman, she actually began to nurse the infant who would become the grandfather of King David (Ruth 4:16-17). Usually, nursing infants belong to young women, certainly not old ladies but the timing was changed because of redemption.

Redemption says it's not too late or too early to experience redemption in the hour that says "no."

Relationship with Jesus trumps the natural order of everything else. Jesus likes to prove that, and does so often.

The **BIG** Headline from Chapter 13

When Jesus brings redemption into time, it is because of relationship.

What This Means to You

Because you are redeemed, time is supposed to work for you and not against you. He can actually change the timing of things to happen sooner or later, faster or slower.

He may in one moment say, "It is not time for this to happen," but you interact with Him. Relationship and favor may cause Him the next moment to change your water into wine.

King Jesus is willing to enter time, bring redemption, and not only change the timeline, but He has proven He is also willing to change the timing of what happens in the timeline.

Questions to Ponder

How does relationship work in redemption?

Who is the miracle of redemption for?

14

Accessing the Exchange Between the Curse of Time and the Freedom of Redemption

In the first section of this book, we discovered that time, space, and matter are together in perfect continuum. In the second section, we began to learn that this continuum is also tethered with sin and with death.

Time, space, and matter have dominion over anybody or anything that sin and death reign over.

If a brother is not subject to sin, he is not subject to death. That happens with the amazing act of redemption King Jesus Christ gave us at the cross.

If you are like, "Hey, wait a minute. Saved people still keel over and die," the reason our physical bodies still die after we are saved is because our bodies are not yet redeemed. Redemption still has a work to accomplish.

> *Because the creation itself also will be delivered from the bondage of corruption into the glorious liberty of the children of God. For we know that the whole creation groans and labors with birth pangs together until now. Not only that, but we also who have the firstfruits of the Spirit, even we ourselves groan within ourselves, eagerly waiting for the adoption, the redemption of our body.*
>
> —Romans 8:21-23

If you are a believer, your spirit is 100 percent redeemed, your mind is in the process of being redeemed, and your body someday will be redeemed. The reason the funeral business is booming is because our bodies are not yet redeemed.

We all avoid the second death because of redemption (Revelation 20:14, 21:8, 2:11, 20:6; Jude 1:12). And some of us will even avoid the first death at the rapture.

> *Behold! I tell you a mystery. We shall not all sleep, but we shall all be changed, in a moment, in the twinkling of an eye, at the last trumpet. For the trumpet will sound, and the dead will be raised imperishable, and we shall be changed. For this perishable body must be put on the imperishable, and this mortal body must put on immorality.*
>
> —1 Corinthians 15:51-53
> (The Pastor Troy Translation)

Right now, your spirit and some parts of your mind are not subject to sin, death, time, space, or matter. As long as time exists, there is still a work of redemption left to be performed.

The physics and logistics of the Spirit is all about faith.

Since we can't go back in time and apply His physical blood to our physical bodies and lives, we have access to His blood and His redeeming life by faith.

Faith is the "one stop shop" and fits-all-tool God gives us to bypass physical limitations.

> *For it is by grace* [the power of God] *you have been saved,* [redeemed] *through faith* [believing and trusting in Him]—*and this is not from yourselves, it is the gift of God.*
>
> —Ephesians 2:8 NIV

We believe all this as Christians. Certainly, no Christian believes we have missed out on our redemption because we were not there in right location and time. We believe faith supersedes all of that. Jesus brought us redemption and faith to give us access to redemption.

Before Jesus went to the cross as the Lamb who takes away the sins of the world, there had to be a physical sacrifice of a physical animal. You had to lay your physical hands on the animal to physically impart your sins into it. Then the animal would be slain and the physical blood of the innocent lamb would be sprinkled onto a burning altar and changed into physical smoke before the Lord.

Today, we access the redemptive blood of Jesus not by physical means but by faith. Jesus did what He did by faith. We access what He did by the same means—faith.

Jesus' death on the cross and His resurrection proved that sin and death do not have control of us. The act of Jesus on the cross provides everything we need for redemption.

> *For we know that our old self was crucified with him so that the body ruled by sin might be done away with, that we should no longer be slaves to sin.*
>
> —Romans 6:6 NIV

There's a Reason Jesus Calls it Being "Born Again"

A big part of the definition of Christian redemption includes being born again. A new experience and a new way of experiencing everything. This is transformation and renewal. Jesus paid the ransom and took on the punishment for our sin so that we can be saved. Just ask Nicodemus. He was an eyewitness to the majesty of Jesus.

> *Now there was a Pharisee, a man named Nicodemus who was a member of the Jewish ruling council. He came to Jesus at night and said, "Rabbi, we know that you are a teacher who has come from God. For no one could perform the signs you are doing if God were not with him."*
>
> *Jesus replied, "Very truly I tell you, no one can see the kingdom of God unless they are born again."*
>
> *"How can someone be born when they are old?" Nicodemus asked. "Surely they cannot enter a second time into their mother's womb to be born!"*

> *Jesus answered, "Very truly I tell you, no one can enter the kingdom of God unless they are born of water and the Spirit. Flesh gives birth to flesh, but the Spirit gives birth to spirit. You should not be surprised at my saying, 'You must be born again.' The wind blows wherever it pleases. You hear its sound, but you cannot tell where it comes from or where it is going. So it is with everyone born of the Spirit."*
>
> —JOHN 3:1-8 NIV

I would argue that Nicodemus was on the right track but the wrong train when he asked, "How can someone be born when they are old?"

Jesus not only gave this old preacher the answer—*"Flesh gives birth to flesh, but the Spirit gives birth to spirit"*—He *was* and *is* the answer. Nicodemus witnessed the cross and I'd like to think he may have even been in that upper room when the Holy Spirit showed up and everyone present was actually born again—the entire timeline was redeemed. Just like the un-dyeing of a red cloth, they were supernaturally made white as snow.

Being born again is the foundation of our faith.

> *Being born again, not of corruptible seed, but of incorruptible, by the word of God, which liveth and abideth forever.*
>
> —1 PETER 1:23 KJV

Faith in Jesus brings His redemption into our lives and conquers sin and death upon our behalf. Now Jesus has dominion over us and death no longer does.

If you don't know, the New Life Version (NLV), a translation of the Bible available since 1969, is one of the most understandable Bible translations without sacrificing accuracy. Take a moment to read through Romans chapter 3 on how Paul teaches the Gentiles about how the covenant of redemption works:

> *But now God has made another way to make men right with Himself. It is not by the Law. The Law and the early preachers tell about it. Men become right with God by putting their trust in Jesus Christ. God will accept men if they come this way. All men are the same to God. For all men have sinned and have missed the shining-greatness of God. Anyone can be made right with God by the free gift of His loving-favor. It is Jesus Christ Who bought them with His blood and made them free from their sins. God gave Jesus Christ to the world. Men's sins can be forgiven through the blood of Christ when they put their trust in Him. God gave His Son Jesus Christ to show how right He is. Before this, God did not look on the sins that were done. But now God proves that He is right in saving men from sin. He shows that He is the One Who has no sin. God makes anyone right with Himself who puts his trust in Jesus.*
>
> —Romans 3:21-26 NLV

Some bullet points to ponder on redemption:

- Jesus redeemed us because God truly does love us (Psalm 44:26, 103:4, 130:7; Isaiah 54:8; Revelation 1:5).

- Redemption belongs to those who trust in Him in repentance (Nehemiah 1:10; Psalm 34:22, 74:2; Isaiah 1:27, 59:20).
- Redemption means the price is remembered and our sins are no longer remembered (Psalm 130:8; Isaiah 44:22; Colossians 1:13-14; Titus 2:14; Hebrews 9:15).
- When you are redeemed, you are owned by the Redeemer. Nothing else is allowed to own you. When we call Him Lord, we are expressing His ownership over our lives (Ephesians 1:13-14, 4:30).
- Redemption is not just for your eternal spirit but also for your physical body (Romans 8:23).
- Redemption is not just for your physical body but also for your emotional soul (Job 33:28; Psalm 34:22, 49:8,15, 55:18, 69:18, 71:23; Lamentations 3:58).
- Redemption doesn't just deliver you in spirit, body, and soul, it can actually be applied to your circumstances and situations in life (Psalm 25:22 says, *"Redeem Israel, O God, out of all their troubles"*).
- What redemption does is pay the terrible price so that what was enslaved can be set free in every way a person can be set free.
- When redemption is applied to anything, the "person, place, or thing" is transformed from

> something experiencing loss to something experiencing gain.

Jesus our Redeemer has a high agenda to personally bring us freedom. When we receive Him, He comes into our space and time to bring us redemption.

The **BIG** Headline from Chapter 14

The very act of being "born again" is redeeming time.

Faith brings us to the Redeemer. Receiving redemption into our time and space comes by faith.

What This Means to You

Your faith is your supernatural key, giving you the open door you need for redemption.

The physical location and condition you are in does not limit your ability to find redemption.

The when of your timeline does not limit your ability to find redemption.

The what of your condition has no determination if redemption can find you and change everything.

If what you are is guilty, it doesn't matter. Faith matters.

> *For God so loved the world that he gave his one and only Son, that whoever believes in him shall not perish but have eternal life. For God did not send his Son into the world to condemn the world, but to save the world through him. Whoever believes in him is not condemned, but whoever does not believe stands*

> *condemned already because they have not believed in the name of God's one and only Son.*
>
> —John 3:16-18 NIV

If what you have made is furniture in hell, your faith can find redemption there.

> *If I ascend into heaven, You are there; If I make my bed in hell, behold, You are there.*
>
> —Psalm 139:8

If what you are is a failure, redemption can still make you a winner. Even make everybody win.

> *I say then, have they stumbled that they should fall? Certainly not! But through their fall, to provoke them to jealousy, salvation has come to the Gentiles. Now if their fall is riches for the world, and their failure riches for the Gentiles, how much more their fullness!*
>
> —Romans 11:11-12

I could go on and on, but the bottom line is this: you don't consult your time, your place, or your circumstances to see if you can access redemption. You find your faith.

Questions to Ponder

With the new information I have about time and redemption, do I have the faith to access the revelation of redeeming my timeline?

Is being "born again" or "saved," in fact, an act of redemption? How has it worked in my life?

How has my worldview of time changed through these chapters?

What is the most surprising revelation on time in these chapters so far?

Section Four

REDEEMING THE TIMES OF YOUR LIFE

Where could I go from your Spirit?
Where could I run and hide from your face?
If I go up to heaven (eternity), you're there!
If I go down to the realm of the dead (also eternity), you're there too!
If I fly with wings into the shining dawn (the future), you're there!
If I fly into the radiant sunset (my past), you're there waiting!

Psalm 139:7-9 TPT

Why would Jesus be waiting for you in your past? Because He wants you to actually find the revelation of redeeming time. He wants to heal your yesterday to bring you a better today and tomorrow.

15

When You Change It Back Then, It Changes Your *Now*

PREMISE 4

You can introduce redemption into any part of your timeline and it changes everything within the timeline including space and matter.

In order to get to the actual practice of redeeming time, we have been walking through three basic premises. Remember, a premise is when you follow a line of logic that will support a conclusion—the Bible calls that a "therefore." It means from there you move forward. Let's review the first three premises before jumping off into the deep end of our fourth crazy cool premise.

> **Premise 1**—God created time. He is not subject to or shackled by it in ay way.
>
> **Premise 2**—God created time for the purpose of works of redemption.
>
> **Premise 3**—Redemption changes everything.

Now that we're cooking with gas, let me blow your mind with the next truth I've found about Jesus the time traveler and His amazing creation called the time-space continuum.

> **Premise 4**—You can introduce redemption into any part of your timeline and it changes everything within the timeline including space and matter.

Everybody knows John 3:16 as the greatest redemptive verse in the Bible, but have you ever read Joshua 3:16? It's another great verse about redemption. It's the verse talking about the Jordan River going dry and the "impossible barrier" that would keep God's people from the going into the land of promise.

> *Then the water flowing down from above stood and rose up in one place far away at Adam, the city beside Zarethan. The water flowing down toward the sea of the Arabah, the Salt Sea, was all cut off. So the people crossed beside Jericho.*
>
> —JOSHUA 3:16 NLV

The miracle didn't just happen at the place where they were crossing. The miracle actually happened at a place called Adam and proceeded to the place where they were—and beyond.

This is prophetic typology for not just the flow of the river but actually for the flow of time going all the way back to the time of Adam. Once the miracle of His presence was applied there, it enabled God's people to cross over in their now—their promise.

Note: when you bring redemption into a past time frame, it will remove impossible barriers and chains that keep you from God's promises in your right now.

Joshua chapter 3 has only 17 verses, and I encourage you to go there and read it until you understand the story in relational revelation.

It's not just a true account, it is also a pattern showing us how to bring redemption into past time frames that will bring a "wonder" into our right now. You can bring a miracle in your past timeline, in fact all the way back to Adam, that will flow back toward where you are right now and release you to cross over into a place you have never been before.

There are so many barriers that keep us from living in the victory of God's promises. The problem is not just that they are impossible to cross but they flow from places impossible to reach. Some examples might look like this:

- You can't cross over into confidence because of the fear that flows from your last divorce.
- You can't cross over into sexual purity and intimate trust because of what flows from the times when you were molested as a child.
- You can't cross over into honor and worth because of what flows from shameful choices you have made.
- Maybe you can't cross over into a life of happiness because of what flows from the death of a loved one.

I am not saying those things are no big deal. I am also not saying you can go back into time and change that; but my friend, I have great news. *Jesus is a time traveler.* He is not subject to time. I am saying He can bring redemption into that moment and it will change the curse to a blessing, right now. It's like backing up the flow of the curse that prohibits you from crossing into your promised places—all the way back to Adam or the point of origin!

Rehash

We have already discovered God is not subject to time, and that God can change and manipulate time. We know time, space, and matter are in continuum, and when redemption is applied to matter it is called a miracle or a wonder.

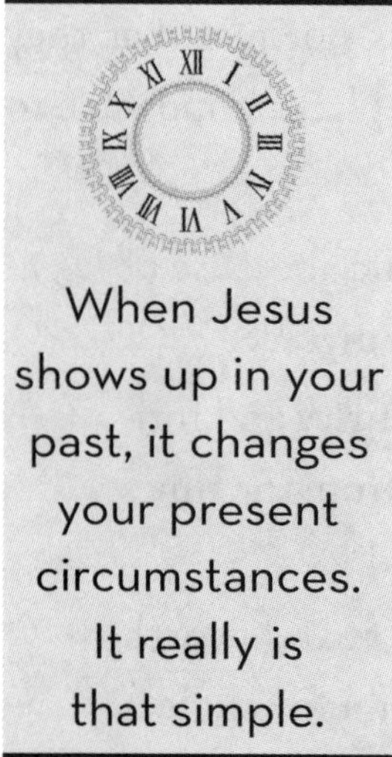

When Jesus shows up in your past, it changes your present circumstances. It really is that simple.

We know the blood of Jesus brings healing, which also means redemption changes matter.

We also know Jesus can step into any place in time He wants or, get this, we invite Him into by faith.

We know there is a difference between redeemed time and unredeemed time. In unredeemed time we experience nothing but great loss. However, in redeemed time, we experience great gain.

So, what do we do with all this new knowledge? We can apply the blood of Jesus to any single event in our past. Once the presence of God is there, it will change our timeline from unredeemed to redeemed. When that time is redeemed, our experience changes from loss to gain.

You already know you can invite Jesus to be made manifest in your right now. Now, you are beginning to understand you can invite Jesus to be made manifest into your "back then" and it will change things in your "right now."

When Jesus shows up in your past, it changes your present circumstances. It really is that simple.

In the crossing of the Jordan River, God made a change (held back the waters) all the way back at a place called Adam to bring a change (dry land) for Joshua and the Hebrews to cross into their place of promise. Do you see it?

How exactly did this work?

Number one, they had to *see* the Ark of the Covenant (the presence of God), measure the space between them, and be prepared to be led by it into a place they had never been before. Read it carefully:

> *So it was, after three days, that the officers went through the camp; and they commanded the people, saying, "When you see the ark of the covenant of the Lord your God, and the priests, the Levites, bearing it, then you shall set out from your place and go after it. Yet there shall be a space between you and it, about two thousand cubits by measure. Do not come near it, that you may know the way by which you must go, for you have not passed this way before."*
>
> —Joshua 3:2-4

Verse 3 in essence says, "When you begin to see His presence...go after it." This is something you pursue. It's not a science. It's completely relational and even though there is a big space between you and that place where you are now, seeing the presence of the Lord (the Ark of the Covenant) will change your impossible barrier.

All prophetic things are things you go after. Things you reach for. Things you practice.

The **BIG** Headline from Chapter 15

When you invite Jesus to redeem your past, it totally changes how you experience your now.

What This Means to You

We have spent fifteen chapters taking a deep look into the reality of how God interacts with time and how we can invite Jesus to bring His redeeming power to change everything.

You can simply invite His visible awesomeness, glory, or manifest presence into any nonredeemed place in your timeline. If You see Him there in that place, you will see a curse change to a blessing. You will instantly see what flows from that past place into your right now place is life instead of death. A river of life in the river of time.

Questions to Ponder

What happens when Jesus shows up in your past?

How does redemption change space and matter?

How is the holding back of the waters on the Jordan all the way back to the village of Adam a picture of redeeming time all the way back to the fall of Adam?

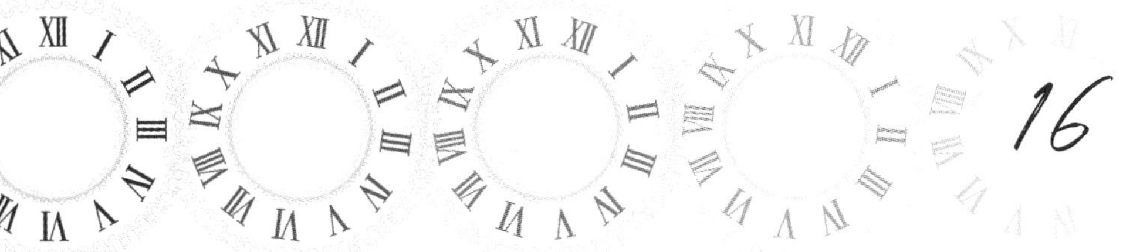

16

Marking the Distance

Let's go back to science and physics for a moment. After this chapter, we actually begin to practice and exercise our ability to redeem time.

Remember, you can't separate time and space. That's why Einstein came up with the single word "spacetime." We measure the distance of stars in terms of time—light years. Because the distance, or the space, is so vast, we actually have a greater grasp on understanding the time.

I call home all the time and tell Leanna, "I'm crossing the county line and I'm about 20 minutes from the ranch." I'm using time to give definition to space or distance. It's actually a common practice among us whether we realize it or not.

The speed of light is 186,000 miles per second or roughly 670 million miles per hour. If you want to travel to the moon, it takes about a second-and-a-half at light speed. Travel to the sun at light speed takes about eight minutes. Can you even imagine? Traveling at a speed where you cross nearly 200,000 miles every second for eight full minutes would only get you to the center of our solar system.

There is a lot of space—a lot of distance—out there, so there's a lot of time and matter out there. It's crazy to think that our giant sun is a dwarf star and every single star you see with your naked eye is much bigger than our star.

If you and I are sitting at the same table across from each other, the reason there is distance is because it takes time for me to get from my chair over to yours. If you get rid of the distance you get rid of the time.

But for now, we don't want to get rid of time. *Time was created for the purpose of transformation that comes through redemption.*

In fact, we want to understand and use time in a way that gives God glory and works for the Kingdom.

In the previous chapter, we learned that the Lord commanded the Israelites to mark the distance between them and the Ark of the Covenant.

> *Yet there shall be a space between you and it, about two thousand cubits by measure.*
>
> —Joshua 3:4

If we are going to introduce redemption into our timeline that goes all the way back to a faraway place called Adam, we need to learn to measure the distance, or the time.

When Abraham was about to offer Isaac as a sacrifice, the Bible says in Genesis 22:4, *"Then on the third day Abraham lifted his eyes and saw the place afar off."*

The mountain where the lamb would be sacrificed was not far off in distance. It was actually far off in time. He even saw the lamb of God there and declared it in verse 13.

How far off? Just about 2,000 years. That brings us back to God telling the children of Israel they had to see the Ark of His presence 2,000 cubits out. I think God was referring back to the prophetic time hop Abraham did on his march up to Mount Moriah (Golgotha). It also refers to the amount of time, two thousand years, the early Church would look for the return of King Jesus.

I believe the cross is what Abraham saw. He would find a ram on the top of his mountain to sacrifice instead of his son, but redemption through God's Son is what he witnessed on the third day. Even though Abraham was seeing it 2,000 years into the future, it was going to cause a miracle that went all the way back to Adam.

You see, Abraham found redemption when he saw Jesus in the timeline of his future, and it brought faith to him in his right now. The Bible says in Hebrews 11:8,17, *"By faith Abraham...."*

Redemption changes everything, not just in time but for all time, no matter where you are in time.

Stopping the Clock

David walked in grace a thousand years before Jesus offered it to the rest of the world. Relationship trumps dispensation.

Moses knew about time, space, and matter thousands of years before the rest of the world did (Genesis 1:1). Experiencing God relationally causes you to understand things way ahead of your own generation.

> *Oh, taste and see that the Lord is good...!*
>
> —Psalm 34:8

Taste is experiencing. Seeing is perception. The point is, how you encounter God and access His redemptive power is much bigger than anything that has ever happened or ever will happen in your timeline.

Taste is experiencing. Seeing is perception.

The eternal blood enters into the temporal timeline and everything changes! If the power of the cross is applied to a past place in your timeline, it changes the right now on the upper timeline.

A Blind Man Sees

John 9:1 says, *"Now as Jesus passed by, He saw a man who was blind from birth."* This is something that goes all the way back to the day the man was born, and John chapter 9 refers to the day he was born six times while describing the events of healing.

> *And His disciples asked Him, saying, "Rabbi, who sinned, this man or his parents, that he was born blind?" Jesus answered, "Neither this man nor his parents sinned, but that the works of God should be revealed in him."*
>
> —JOHN 9:2-3

When Jesus added to the day the man was born, it instantly brought a miracle into his right now day. He was healed of his blindness from his birth!

A Woman Is Healed

In Matthew 9:20-22, Mark 5:25-34, and Luke 8:42-48, there is a timeline that goes 12 years back. A woman who has been slowly bleeding to death, which also made her ritually unclean and untouchable in Jewish culture, dares to reach out to Jesus for healing.

When redemption was brought into the day she started to bleed, she was instantly healed on her current day. She accessed redemption by touching the timeless Redeemer.

A Good Friend Is Raised from the Dead

Before Lazarus came waddling out of the tomb (or jumping out like a guy in a potato sack race), the terrible disappointment his sisters dealt with was the timing of Jesus.

> *Now Martha said to Jesus, "Lord, if You had been here, my brother would not have died. But even now I know that whatever You ask of God, God will give You." Jesus said to her, "Your brother will rise again."*
>
> —John 11:21-23

Then Jesus said these important words:

> *I am the resurrection and the life. He who believes in Me, though he may die, he shall live. And whoever lives and believes in Me shall never die. Do you believe this?*
>
> —John 11:25-26

Jesus was saying, "It's not about a day. It's about Me! I Am greater than any measure of time whether it was four days ago when Lazarus died or thousands of years in the future when he rises out of the ground. I Am the resurrection. I Am life, and I Am what you are waiting for. Not a day. Not a year. You are waiting for Me to step into time—and I Am here, right now!"

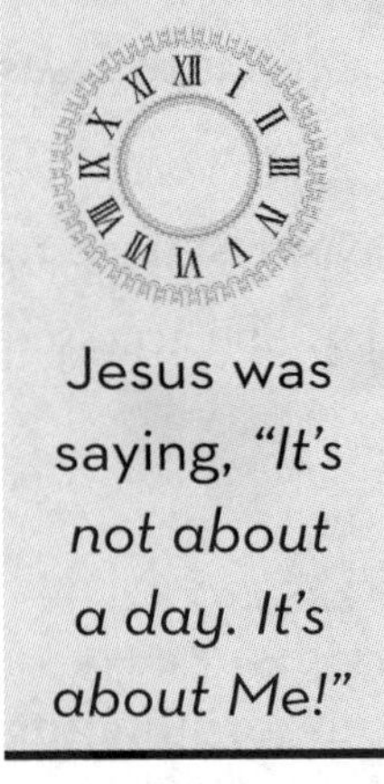
Jesus was saying, *"It's not about a day. It's about Me!"*

I think He is still saying that to all of us today.

It's not about the drama of the day anymore. You're going to make it all about Him—and that's going to change everything.

The **BIG** Headline from Chapter 16

It's not about a day or an hour. It's about Jesus showing up. He is the Way, the Truth, and the Life—not the segment of time.

What This Means to You

You can experience the reality of something in Jesus that is otherwise impossible within time.

If time says, "It's a long way off," you can bring it into your right now with the King of kings in your now. You don't serve a day. You serve the One who owns the day and brings a different timing.

Then he said to them, "The Sabbath was made for man, not man for the Sabbath. So the Son of Man is Lord even of the Sabbath."

—MARK 2:27-28 NIV

Questions to Ponder

Pastor Troy believes Abraham saw the cross of Jesus through space and time when he was on Mount Moriah. Do I agree with his theory? Why or why not?

How is resurrection an example of redeeming time?

SECTION FOUR SUMMARY

What We have Learned so Far

Check the box when you think you have a mental grip and peace in your heart on each point.

- ☐ Redemption is the act of buying something back, or paying a price or ransom to return something to your possession.
- ☐ Redemption is a term used for freeing someone from slavery.
- ☐ Redemption changes ownership.
- ☐ Premise 3: Redemption changes everything, not just over time but for all time.
- ☐ The price of redemption that out-values and out-weighs everything is the blood of Jesus. His pure,

holy, and uncontaminated life triumphs over all things created.

- ☐ The mission statement of Jesus in Luke 4:18 is to bring redemption, meaning to bring deliverance from evil by payment of a price.
- ☐ The results and benefits of redemption are all definitions of goodness, life, prosperity, freedom, honor, and victorious living.
- ☐ Redemption changes common things into extraordinary things as the water was turned into wine.
- ☐ Redemption changes a curse into a blessing.
- ☐ Redemption changes everything once and for all (Hebrews 9:12). That doesn't just mean for now, but for past, present, and future.
- ☐ All of the physical miracles recorded in the Bible are the result of redemption changing matter.
- ☐ If you can bring redemption in to change matter, you can also bring it into time and space. You can redeem your time the same way you can redeem your physical circumstances.
- ☐ When Jesus brings redemption into time, He also changes the timing of things.
- ☐ Everything in the Kingdom is relational before it is functional.
- ☐ When Jesus brings redemption into the common messes of humanity, He tends to change the timing of how it usually goes. He will even reverse the way things always happen.

- ☐ Redemption says it's not too late or even too early to experience redemption in the hour that says no.
- ☐ If you are a believer, your spirit is 100 percent redeemed, your mind is in the process of being redeemed, and your body someday will be redeemed.
- ☐ Since we can't go back in time and apply His physical blood to our physical bodies and lives, we have access to His blood and His redeeming life by faith.
- ☐ Since we can't go back in time to messed-up parts of our lives and fix things, we can access those time frames by bringing redemption by faith.
- ☐ Premise 4—You can introduce redemption into any part of your timeline and it changes everything within the timeline including space and matter. If you can bring redemption into a place in time past, what flows from that place into your right now is completely different. Your right now is instantly changed.
- ☐ When Jesus shows up in your past, it changes your present circumstances. It is really that simple.
- ☐ It's not about a day, it's all about King Jesus. Jesus proved that to Martha by resurrecting her brother before the day of resurrection. There is no need to depend upon a day when you can depend upon your relationship with Jesus.

A Prayer for Redeeming Your Time

King Jesus, You are my Kinsman Redeemer, my Holy Lamb of sacrifice, and my Mighty Lion of Judah who roars into my life. Bring redemption into my every hour and every time frame.

Jesus, in the place where I have been alone, I invite You to be made manifest and cause me to see You instead of the day. In the days I have been shamed and convicted of guilt, I invite You to bring the Lamb and the Lion of Your presence to cause me to see You instead of seeing the day. Let my flow of time and experience change from that moment until now with honor instead of shame, and holiness instead of guilt.

On the days I was heartbroken, confused, and upset, I now invite You into those past time frames and declare Your goodness, sanity, and stability because I see You there! I declare that nothing from my past shall become a toxin in my present or jeopardize my future because I now see the glory of the Lord in all my times!

I repent of any lie I have spoken, believed, or acted upon that accused You of not being with me. You have never left me! Your glory is greater than any failure of the day. Your redemption is more powerful than any slavery that chained me. I am free by the blood of the Lamb and the word of my testimony in this time, and all for time, because Jesus makes it so!

Amen!

"There is never a wrong time to make the right decision. The time is always right to do what is right."

—Dr. Martin Luther King Jr.

PREMISE 5

We are stewards—not owners —of our lives. As priests, we apply the blood. As kings, we bring Kingdom dominion into all we steward including time.

In this section you will learn about:

- How to redeem your time
- How to change your time from a curse to a blessing
- Redeeming a time of tragedy and loss
- Stewarding the impact and managing the change through proper response
- Redeeming a time of shame and dishonor
- Redeeming times of wasted years or lost investment
- Redeeming times of great failure
- Redeeming times of bondage
- Redeeming times of great injustice
- Redeeming times you were absent for people you should have been there for and vice versa
- Redeeming times of lost opportunity
- Redeeming the times of family in times way past
- Redeeming time past, time present, and time future

Section Five

BEING A KING AND A PRIEST OF YOUR TIME

The Supernatural Act of Changing Your Time to Glorify King Jesus

17

Redeeming Time

Let's get to the business of making this happen. Now you know and have carefully considered the following premises:

Premise 1—God created time. He is not subject to or shackled by it in any way.

Premise 2—God created time for the purpose of works of redemption.

Premise 3—Redemption changes everything.

Premise 4—You can introduce redemption into any part of your timeline and it changes everything within the timeline including space and matter.

Finally, we come to:

Premise 5—We are stewards—not owners—of our lives. As priests, we apply the blood. As kings, we bring Kingdom dominion into all we steward including time. We bring redemption in the time frame and walk in power and dominion from the redeemed place.

Kings and Priests

Revelation 1:6 (KJV) says, *"And hath made us kings and priests unto God and his Father; to him be glory and dominion for ever and ever. Amen."*

Notice that this is for all time!

Revelation 5:10 (NIV) says, *"You have made them to be a kingdom and priests to serve our God, and they will reign on the earth."*

Notice this is for right now!

You and I are held responsible for how we accept the invitation, follow the command to apply the blood, and bring Kingdom dominion to all God has trusted us with. How is it we do not believe this applies to His precious gift of time?

Now that you know how created time works, what it is for, and how the Lord interacts with time, hopefully you know how God interacts with you as well.

> *Ask, and it will be given to you; seek, and you will find; knock, and it will be opened to you.*
>
> —Matthew 7:7

Let's do this.

Activating Redemption into Your Time Frames

So here is what you do:

1. Ask the Holy Spirit to search your heart and your entire timeline. Give Him full disclosure

of your life—the good, the bad, the ugly, the grand—all of it. (See Scriptures on searching the times in your life in Section Five.)

2. There will be certain markers within your life where you still experience terrible loss and pain. These are the places you are going to invite the Lord Jesus Christ to be made manifest in that unredeemed epic event or that season. (See Scriptures on identifying markers and places that need redemption in Section Five.)
3. Invite God into that place. Repent and ask Him to have total dominion in that very place. Ask the Lord to show you His presence in that place. Finding Jesus there will change everything for you. (See Scriptures on inviting His manifest presence and glory into your space-time in Section Five.)
4. Claim and declare your redemption. (See Scriptures on declarations and redemption in Section Five.)
5. Commit your life to living from victory in that place because of the blood of the Lamb and the power of redemption. (See Scriptures on vows, commitment to victory, and redemption in Section Five.)
6. Celebrate your freedom and make a big deal out of your change. Note the changes that happen in your now because of the redemption Jesus has

brought to that place in time. (See Scriptures on seeing the new thing, acknowledging the Lord, and the prophetic acts of celebration in Section Five.)

7. Live a prophetic and victorious lifestyle dedicated to the contemplation and the celebration of redemption. (See Chapter 20 on stewarding the impact and managing the change of redeeming time.)

18

My Personal Testimony of Redeeming a Time of Great Loss and Tragedy

Scotty McKay was a very good friend of mine. He was my music producer and band manager. Scotty had lived with Elvis in the fifties, several Beatles in the sixties, and the Yard Birds in the seventies. He had played on the Ed Sullivan Show as a teenager. Born Max Lipscomb, Dick Clark renamed him Scotty McKay. He had acted in movies and was something like a major musical hero to me. As already stated, he was my friend.

After writing songs and recording on his last album, *The Morning Side of Midnight,* his first Christian album, we were in the studio producing my Christian rock album. It was a collection of southern rock/country songs that praised Jesus with sounds from my youth.

It was Friday, March 15, 1991. In five short days, he and I would be in Nashville with the legendary producer/artist James E. "Buzz" Cason. We would present our showcase, be directed into management, and off we would go into a signed recording deal and a world tour.

I called Scotty and spoke to him. He was in Dallas at Rosewood Studios working on the last mix before my big listen on Monday.

"Sounds great man," he told me. "This is going to be huge, Troy."

We laughed, made plans, and spoke about the radio play of his song, "The Price has been Paid."

This song, that was climbing the charts, was actually my song and my voice that had been labeled incorrectly. Christian radio stations in Holland and several European countries were playing it big. It wasn't a game-changer for our friendship, but it was something we were trying to correct. Scotty was making sure that he made things right with me and my music career. Something much better was going to happen for me.

"It's going to be crazy, man. Buzz has really set us up in Nashville," he promised me.

I was so excited. I was so hopeful for our future and convinced I would be able to play stadiums and travel the world praising King Jesus. There was no doubt that the timing of all this was going to be perfect.

A Different Day Later

Before driving all the way to McKinny, I called Scotty on Monday morning. I couldn't reach him so I called out to Rosewood to see if he was there.

The guy on the phone told me Scotty was not there. He was dead from a heart attack.

In shock, I told him I didn't believe him. Scotty was playing a joke on me.

"I'm not joking," he said coldly. "Scotty is dead. I know you've got a showcase in Nashville this week. If you want your tape, you need to know Scotty has not paid me yet."

In the confusion of trying to process what was happening, I remembered the last thing Scotty told me before he said he loved me and hung up the phone.

"I just ate some bad Mexican food, man. I got serious heartburn."

Instead of praying for him, I made fun of him because he was old. Scotty was an elderly 51. I was 24 and 51 seemed ancient to me. It all swirled in my young brain. I immediately got sick and started bawlin' and squalin' as we say here in Texas.

The agreement Scotty had with Buzz Cason died with Scotty. I paid over $4,000 for the two-inch recording tape from the studio. This was the year before everything went digital and I haven't heard it since 1991. My music career never really happened and Scotty died alone as he told me he feared he would.

I went into mourning and just plain freaked out at the horrible feeling of loss and regret. It was a tragic loss. I believed I would never get over the terrible ending of something beautiful if I had not learned to redeem the time.

New Beginnings

This was the very first time I asked God to redeem a certain moment in time. At his funeral, I was so overcome with grief—first at the fact that he died alone. Second at the fact that this was the moment I was supposed to be in Nashville launching my music career. Instead, I was grieving at his grave.

I cried all the way there. I cried in the parking lot. I cried during the service. I couldn't even drive home I was so devastated. When I got home to my little shack out in the middle of nowhere, I walked in the back 400 acres of cow fields under the midnight stars.

"Lord, I can't stand it that Scotty was alone when he died," I wept and moaned. "He didn't want to die alone!"

Suddenly, a supernatural moment of clarity hit me as the still, small, yet thunderous whisper of King Jesus said, "Ask Me to be with him and I will answer your prayer. Trust Me to be with him, Troy, and I will show you I AM."

I instantly knew that though I was subject to the flow of time, Jesus was not. Though the event was in present/past tense for me, it held no limitation to King Jesus.

I immediately asked God to be with Scotty in the final moments of his life and to make His presence manifest to him. I asked God to make his last moments the most remarkable and best moments of his life because of his encounter with Jesus. I began to declare instead of fear, God would give Scotty confidence and peace. I rebuked pain and prophesied the comfort of the Holy Spirit. I did this as if I was there, with faith knowing that God was introducing Himself into that time frame.

Even though it was past tense for me, I knew it wasn't for God. I also supernaturally knew that God had answered my prayer in my past because He had faith that I would pray this prayer in the future. I knew it!

At that moment, everything changed. My entire experience of this tragic and horrible loss changed as if I had moved from the back of the plane into first class. The same plane but an entirely different experience in this plane.

The Lord showed me, and I saw it. I felt how He was faithful to be with Scotty when he died. His ending was glorious and his transition into eternity full of laughter and joy. I saw it!

Redemption Made Manifest from the Flow of Time

That's been almost thirty years ago and I still miss Scotty. I know I am closer to seeing him again now than ever before, but not until redemption has run its course.

I can mark and acknowledge so many miracles that have happened from this once tragic event. The event still happened, but what stems from it is a blessing instead of a curse because of the power of Jesus and the prophetic act of redeeming time.

Even though my music career was tragically stolen by death, the benefits of redemption have seen to it I have lived life as if that never happened. It continues even today.

- I pastor an enormous church and can lead worship in front of thousands anytime I feel the need to.

- I play at my leisure with amazing professional musicians and worshipping warriors whom I love with all my heart.
- I have traveled to 58 countries and led worship on five different continents.
- I have played full blown stadium events in India and in my hometown of Fort Worth, Texas, at the Fort Worth Convention Center.
- I have played before literal kings in Uganda including His Majesty Oyo Nyimba Kabamba Iguru Rukidi IV, King of the Tooro Kingdom.
- I have heard my songs played on BBC Radio England and have been reviewed in magazines worldwide.
- I played lead guitar on a song I wrote titled "Advent." It's the opening song to my TV show *The OpenDoor Experience*, seen weekly in more than 200 nations on several worldwide networks.
- I wrote a song titled "Here I Am." It plays in the background of the beginning of my podcasts and radio programs. That means I have a song on 74 radio stations, four times a day across the United States!

Not bad for a guy who had his music career stolen by the tragic and untimely death of a close friend some 30 years ago.

This is only one of many amazing stories of being set free from a terrible situation or moment of time. This is one true account of so many where my Redeemer found me in a cursed place and blessed me from there.

> *Let the redeemed of the Lord say so, whom He has redeemed from the hand of the enemy.*
>
> —Psalm 107:2

When you bring the manifest Redeemer into a tragic or terrible time, what flows from that time forward is redemption. I will continue to reap the benefits of redemption from that once terrible and tragic hour, all the days of my life. I would not be surprised if I still have a number-one hit song yet to be manifest.

I have no more musical pursuits or ambition, but I do expect I will taste and see that the Lord is good. Surely goodness and mercy will follow me all the days of my life in this one category from the very moment my Redeemer stepped into it on March 17, 1991.

The ground-breaking news here is it's never too late to bring the Redeemer into a time frame of a tragic event of terrible loss. Even if it is hours, days, years, or even decades in your time past.

God is not subject to time. Time is subject to Him.

Our Redeemer lives.

The **BIG** Headline from Chapter 18

Jesus can redeem and change the time of your terrible place of tragedy and loss.

What This Means to You

Not only will your experience of the event itself change because you find King Jesus there, the results flowing from that tragic event will also completely change. From the time of loss, you can actually experience gain because of redemption.

Remember the definition of redemption from Chapter 11: "Redemption is the act of buying something back or paying a price or ransom to return something to your possession. Redemption is the English translation of the Greek word *agorazo,* meaning 'to purchase in the marketplace.' In ancient times, it often referred to the act of buying a slave. It carried the meaning of freeing someone from chains, prison, or slavery."

Questions to Ponder

How did the story of Pastor Troy's revelation that Jesus wanted to apply redemption to his friend Scotty's last hours affect me?

Does this story give me hope for my own places of pain or failure? Why?

The revelation of redeeming time says the event does not change, but how the event affects me today changes from negative to positive, a curse to a blessing. Is this something I need in my life? Is this something I should share with others as they grapple with guilt, shame, and pain from past wounds?

19

How to Redeem a Tragic Place of Loss in Your Own Life and Timeline

What to Do

1. Find a specific moment in time you experienced great loss from something tragic and wrong.
2. Mark the moment. If possible, find the actual date and present your time before the Lord.
3. Confess your pain, hurt, anger, and any terrible feelings or non-Kingdom thoughts you have expressed or harbored. Refuse to be in agreement with them.
4. Literally invite King Jesus into that moment believing it is not too late for Him and that He is willing to do so. Ask Him to appear in that moment of time and in that physical place.

5. Ask the Holy Spirit to supernaturally cause you to perceive His real and tangible presence there. Ask Him to show you, or speak to you, and tell you how He is there, where He is there, and what He is doing.
6. Praise Him for His manifest presence and for how beautiful He is in showing up in this place. Declare His goodness. Proclaim His redemption and righteousness in that place.
7. Ask God to change what flows from that tragedy to be a blessing instead of a curse. Go after advancement, encouragement, and hope as redemption changes the shift from loss to gain. Death is overcome by life and the presence of King Jesus changes everything.
8. Ask God to let your right now experience change from the tragedy of loss to the blessing from Him being there. From that place in time until now, you have and will continue to be blessed because the Master has redeemed you. Pray for a new time and new flow of time.
9. Be prepared to acknowledge any new way this becomes manifest or true in your life. Any time you are blessed in that category of your life, you have to recognize it, and give God glory that redemption has changed what flows from that time.

In all your ways acknowledge Him, and He shall direct your paths.

—Proverbs 3:6

10. Grow in the skill set of acknowledging and marking the blessings that come from this redeemed place. How you steward this awareness determines your ability to step into more and more.

For I say to you, that to everyone who has will be given; and from him who does not have, even what he has will be taken away from him.

—Luke 19:26

A Prayer for Redeeming the Time of a Tragic Event

(Mark the day. Name what happened.)

King Jesus, I lift up the day of ________________
when ____________________________ *happened.*
This has been a time of great grief and loss for me. I repent for anything I have accused You of concerning this. I am sorry for the problem I have created and the way I have handled it.

(Call upon His manifest presence in that terrible place.)

I ask You, King Jesus, to be with me in that very moment. I ask You, Lord, to cause Your goodness to pass before me in that terrible place and show me

Your glory. It is not too late for You to enter into that moment of time. Please be with me, comfort me, and protect me in that place. You have declared You are willing to redeem me and set me free from the terrible thing that happened.

(Go after the prophetic gift of seeing and personally encountering [tasting] His presence in that place.)

O taste and see that the LORD is good: blessed is the man that trusts in him.

—Psalm 34:8

Holy Spirit, show me the manifest presence of Jesus with me in that place. Show me exactly where He is and what He is doing in that moment of time past. Open my eyes to see Him there and open my ears to hear His words in that place.

(Praise and worship King Jesus in this place.)

I praise You, my God, that Your goodness overcomes this evil. I praise You for Your heart and for Your power. I declare that God was with me then, is with me now, and will be with me in the future.

(Prophetically declare and celebrate.)

I declare I have been redeemed and set free from that terrible thief by the blood of the Lamb. Now let my time change! Let the throne of His presence produce life from that very moment into my right now time, in Jesus' name. Amen.

Be prepared to note and mark the changes that are coming from that redeemed place.

What to Look For

You will feel breakthrough.

You will experience and praise God for the shift.

In any glimpse, or supernatural seeing, declare your sight, and praise God for it.

Be ready for real, tangible change to happen that you can actually measure and mark. It is so important that you steward what you are receiving from this new redeemed flow of time.

This, like all prophetic things and spiritual gifts, is something you exercise, practice, and become skilled at. This is something you do over and over to develop supernatural muscle memory. You intentionally press into these encounters with the Lord and desire to go after such things. Those who are unbelieving, passive, and apathetic never see, hear, or personally experience the amazing things God has for them.

The encounter and the change in time comes from being desperate and dependent upon the Lord.

(See Scriptures on desperation and dependence in Section Five.)

A Miraculous Testimony of Redeeming Time from the Vietnam War

A friend of mine who is a Messianic Jew called me one day and asked me to help him redeem a tragic time that was causing terrible pain decades after.

His wife's brothers and sisters didn't speak to each other and hadn't for years. They lived in different parts of the United States and remained disconnected.

The problem came from a terrible childhood of abuse from an alcoholic father. He would lose his temper over nothing and predictably make everyone miserable and fearful.

As each brother or sister grew and moved out of the house, they went as far away as they could and cut all ties.

My buddy told me the root of the issue. His wife's dad had gone to Vietnam and was injured in a horrific way. He spent nearly a year in the hospital before being shipped home to a beautiful wife and a house full of kids. He was maimed and disfigured for the rest of his life. When he came home, he was not the same man in any way. He didn't even feel like a man because of his injury.

With her father long dead and no way to make this right, my friend said something brilliant, "I would like to invite King Jesus to be with him while he was sitting in the hospital bed for all those months. I want to ask King Jesus to bring His presence into my father-in-law's life back then. I know He can change the timeline to a redeemed one and it will make a huge difference in the results of what happened."

I was blown away at his faith.

So, we did just that. We asked God to take up residence in the life of that man in the hospital in Vietnam back in the early 1960s. We invited King Jesus into that place in time the way I invite Him into my grandkid's classroom or my pulpit when I preach. We asked that this man would not be alone but that

Jesus would touch him, heal him, and redeem him from his horrific injury. We asked the thorns of the unredeemed evil be cut off and the fruit of God's presence to be made evident.

Believe me, this flow of time changed from cursed to redeemed.

Within the next two weeks, every one of his wife's siblings called her from out of the blue! The phone started ringing with a brother or a sister saying, "I've been thinking about you, and we need to get together soon." They connected to have their very first Christmas together, and it was a miraculous reconciliation.

See, with the new timeline came a new history. Even though they all experienced abuse in their timeline, King Jesus presented another timeline with His presence in it. This one came without the shame, loss, and the curse of that terrible trauma because now the presence of the Lord was there.

Redeeming the Time of a Tragic Death—Another Miracle Testimony

A childhood friend had lost her parents in a terrible plane crash. She was only 18 when both of them died. Years later, when we were in our forties, I was talking to her at a local store.

"You know, I have really prayed for you through the years," I told her. "Your parents were good people and I can't even imagine how bad that was for you."

"It's still bad," she said. "It's not just that they never knew my kids or my three husbands," she joked about her messes with relationships. "I have never been able to get over the terrible way they died."

A big tear rolled down her face. "Yeah. It's bad."

Then she shrugged her shoulders, wiped her nose, and changed her voice. "But there's nothing you can do about it. Life sucks then you die, and sometimes it's really, really bad how you die."

I hadn't seen her for years and everything in me was wanting to bring Jesus to her. I hate hopelessness.

"Will you let me be a crazy Jesus freak for a minute and bring hope to you?" I asked.

"Sure. You going to tell me about heaven? I believe in heaven," she said.

"No, I'm going to tell you that Jesus is God and He's not subject to time. If you don't like the way they died, let's ask Jesus to be with them right before they died to bless and comfort them. Let's ask Jesus to be there at the crash with them and let them know He is with them."

"What?" she asked. "You can do that?"

"Yeah, I do it all the time. If I can't be in a place, I ask God to be there. If I can't be in that time, I ask God to be there. Let me show you."

"Wait, what will that do if we pray that prayer—that God would be with them in the crash when they died?" she asked with a spark of hope in her eyes.

"Well, for them it could mean peace and comfort instead of horror and pain," I said. "For you, it might mean a ton of different things God can heal and make right. I don't know. Let's see."

We prayed together and I simply asked God to be manifest in the moments before and during the crash. I asked the Holy

Spirit to give them a heart to know Him and to recognize His presence hours and days before the crash. I asked God to be with them and to bless them in their final moments with His peace and confidence.

"Wow!" she said. Both of us were crying. "I really felt God, like *really* felt like God was with them and me. I don't think that's ever happened before."

Taking a big chance and trusting the Lord, I told her that while I was praying I saw her dad's arm around her mom during the crash. He was loving her and telling her he loved her. I saw a big red ring on his hand.

"That's my dad's college ring. He wore it all the time. How weird," she said, wiping away tears and laughing. "You saw that? Really?"

"Sure did," I told her. "It's wasn't horrible for them. God was with them. I just saw it."

Several months went by and one of the girls who answers the church phone called me to say some crazy lady was in the office. She said this lady was a friend of mine and she really needed to talk to me.

It was my childhood friend. She asked if I remembered what God had showed me when we were redeeming the time of her parents' death. I assured her I remember all of it, the arm, the hand, the ring, and the words they were speaking.

"Well, I have never had the guts to visit the crash site but after our prayer, I started feeling like I could visit it and that it would be all right," she said.

"My brother and I were standing at the very spot, kind of kicking at the ground, and I told him what you had prayed. I told him what you told me you saw. I no sooner told him when I looked down and found this..."

She held up a big red ring laden in gold. She actually found the ring that God had caused me to see in the Spirit. That ring confirmed His redemption.

It changed her life and changed it for good. She knew for certain that God had answered her prayer. The Lord was truly with her parents, way back then, after we prayed 25 years later.

I have since wondered if that ring had been there all the time or only since the time we had prayed. Just fun to think about.

I Repeat, This Is What to Look For!

Be ready for real, tangible change to happen that you can actually measure and mark. When we have a high value for and make a big deal out of something in the Kingdom, this falls under the category of "The Precious Things of Heaven."

> *And of Joseph he said: "Blessed of the Lord is his land, with the precious things of heaven...."*
>
> —Deuteronomy 33:13

The word for *precious* in Hebrew is *meged. Meged* means to be "distinguished" or to be "eminent." Eminent means "to stand out from." It is the Hebrew word for "excellence"!

> *Therefore, to you who believe, He is precious....*
>
> —1 Peter 2:7

20

Stewarding the Impact and Managing the Change

You and I are expected to walk in dominion over the things God brings us. A big part of victorious Kingdom living is learning to maintain and protect the victories—minor and major—God is trusting us with. Our mental and spiritual management of His Kingdom coming into our lives is proven by our willingness to conform to the image of who He is in those places. We also conform to who He says we are in those places.

The following are eight major biblical points and examples (the number 8 represents new beginnings) on the importance of learning how to recognize and respond to the miracles of redeeming time.

1. When Jesus does a miracle, we are held accountable for how that encounter impacts and changes our lives. That's on us and is our responsibility.

> *Woe to you, Chorazin! Woe to you, Bethsaida! For if the mighty works which were done in you had been done in Tyre and Sidon, they would have repented long ago, sitting in sackcloth and ashes.*
>
> —Luke 10:13

Jesus was personally offended at the lack of impact His selfless acts of redemption had upon certain cities.

2. When Jesus does a life-changing miracle for us, our wholeness is determined by our willingness to be truly thankful and appreciative. Praise, worship, and giving honor to King Jesus qualifies us for the upgrade of wholeness. The example of the one leper who returned to thank Jesus for his healing is the key here:

   > *And one of them, when he saw that he was healed, turned back, and with a loud voice glorified God, and fell down on his face at his feet, giving him thanks: and he was a Samaritan. And Jesus answering him said, Were there not ten cleansed? but where are the nine? There are not any found that returned to give glory to God, save this stranger. And he said unto him, Arise, go thy way: thy faith hath made thee whole.*
   >
   > —Luke 17:15-19 KJV

Notice the nine lepers who didn't thank Jesus were "cleansed." I believe that means their leprosy was healed. However, the one who returned to praise, worship, and acknowledge his healing was made "whole." What does that mean? I believe his missing limbs were restored. That his timeline was absolutely taken back to his pre-leprous state and he was, indeed, made whole.

3. It is one thing for the Lord to invite us into a privileged and exclusive place, it is totally our responsibility to value His invitation more than our own agenda.

   And Jesus answered and spoke to them again by parables and said: "The kingdom of heaven is like a certain king who arranged a marriage for his son, and sent out his servants to call those who were invited to the wedding; and they were not willing to come. Again, he sent out other servants, saying, 'Tell those who are invited, "See, I have prepared my dinner; my oxen and fatted cattle are killed, and all things are ready. Come to the wedding."' But they made light of it and went their ways, one to his own farm, another to his business.

   —Matthew 22:1-5

4. Some people accept the invitation but accept it on their own terms. It offends the Lord if we experience His gift but do not change accordingly.

   But when the king came in to see the guests, he saw a man there who did not have on a wedding garment. So, he said to him, "Friend, how did you come in here without a wedding garment?" And he was speechless. Then the king said to the servants, "Bind him hand and foot, take him away, and cast him into outer darkness; there will be weeping and gnashing of teeth."

—Matthew 22:11-13

When Jesus invites you into a redeemed place, you have to be willing to change your garments from sackcloth to praise. You have to be willing to live according to a different experience.

It is one thing for God to reveal to you His new plan, it's a whole other thing for you to conform your life to the image of that plan.

5. The Lord will speak a powerful word and do an amazing new thing in your life. However, it is your responsibility to guard what God has done and keep it special in your life. You have to value and make a big deal out this thing and make it special to you personally.

But Mary kept all these things and pondered them in her heart.

—Luke 2:19

Your commitment to hang on to the truth of the Word and the impact of His presence is all about being committed to a life of contemplation. You need to be dedicated to holy thinking. What you meditate or mentally chew on is a skill set developed by people dedicated to holiness and victory.

6. It is one thing for God to do a thing, but it is a whole other thing for us to recognize it, and let it fully impact and influence our lives.

You can be in an incredible place and not know it until Jesus shows you. Even though you know it, it is up to you to make that place different from how you once knew it. This is seen in the Bible as renaming a place.

> *Then Jacob awoke from his sleep and said, "Surely the Lord is in this place, and I did not know it." And he was afraid and said, "How awesome is this place! This is none other than the house of God, and this is the gate of heaven!" Then Jacob rose early in the morning, and took the stone that he had put at his head, set it up as a pillar, and poured oil on top of it. And he called the name of that place Bethel; but the name of that city had been Luz previously.*
>
> —Genesis 28:16-19

7. It is one thing for God to perform a miracle, but it is another thing for you to stop and actually get in front of this miracle. The miracle doesn't change everything until you do.

> *And the Angel of the Lord appeared to him in a flame of fire from the midst of a bush. So he looked, and behold, the bush was burning with fire, but the bush was not consumed. Then Moses said, "I will now turn aside and see this great sight, why the bush does not burn." So when the Lord saw that he turned aside to look, God called to him from the midst of the bush and said, "Moses, Moses!" And he said, "Here I am."*
>
> —Exodus 3:2-4

God didn't speak to Moses by name until he turned aside to see the burning bush. He had to be willing to investigate further the miracle God was doing.

> *It is the glory of God to conceal a matter, but the glory of kings is to search out a matter.*
>
> —PROVERBS 25:2

8. When God tells us to engage in the power of a prophetic act, our measure of victory is determined by our passionate willingness to respond.

> *And Elisha said to him, "Take a bow and some arrows." So he took himself a bow and some arrows. Then he said to the king of Israel, "Put your hand on the bow." So he put his hand on it, and Elisha put his hands on the king's hands. And he said, "Open the east window"; and he opened it. Then Elisha said, "Shoot"; and he shot. And he said, "The arrow of the Lord's deliverance and the arrow of deliverance from Syria; for you must strike the Syrians at Aphek till you have destroyed them. Then he said, "Take the arrows"; so he took them. And he said to the king of Israel, "Strike the ground"; so he struck three times, and stopped. And the man of God was angry with him, and said, "You should have struck five or six times; then you would have struck Syria till you had destroyed it! But now you will strike Syria only three times."*
>
> —2 KINGS 13:15-19

This young king could have seen his kingdom fully delivered from the enemy, but he was too worried about what others thought. He was skeptical and unbelieving. All he had to do was show some faith in the Lord and hit those arrows on the ground over and over again with passion and hope. He didn't and his nation paid for it. God loves a prophetic act, and we tend to walk in power and authority when we understand this.

The **BIG** Headline from Chapter 20

If you want to see true transformation, you must be dedicated to being watchful, recognizing what God is doing, celebrating it, praising Him for it, and conforming your life to the new beginning.

What This Means to You

Jesus gives us this principle in this amazing New Testament verse:

> *Do not give what is holy to the dogs; nor cast your pearls before swine, lest they trample them under their feet, and turn and tear you in pieces.*
>
> —Matthew 7:6

We act like pigs and dogs when we have no value for the precious things of heaven. We even become hostile against the Giver when we find no value for the precious things He is giving us. Be ready to magnify the Lord even in the tiniest shift of time.

21

Redeeming a Time of Great Shame Into a Time of Great Honor

"Here's to the sunny slopes of yesterday."

—Captain Augustus "Gus" McCrae,

Lonesome Dove

The late 1980s were shining times for me. I got saved, involved in full-time ministry, married, and had my first child all from 1986-89. I saw my first miracle, gave my first prophetic word, and made the transition from my teens into my twenties full of the Holy Spirit. I was absolutely fearless with passion and zeal for Jesus.

There is one really bad thing that happened though. It was something I had to have redeemed from just plain sad to just plain hilarious. Further proof of redeeming time.

School's Out

I barely graduated high school in 1985 and I mean barely. If it were not for Brother Mosely and the fundamentalist Baptists at my basically Amish high school, I would not have graduated at all. They worked with me all the way, helping me take my final exam that lasted until almost five o'clock on my graduation day. The ceremony started at seven and I honestly didn't know if I was going to graduate until just before I got on the stage.

Again, this was due to the patience, love, and dedication of my teachers, not because of me. I am forever grateful. I obviously didn't do well in school. I was much more interested in girls, music, rodeo, and drawing cars with fifty engines.

A year later, I found Jesus and immediately became a gifted learner. Part of my faith package included an ability to read, understand, and remember things in a supernatural way. That's the power of the Holy Spirit who taught me all things and brought to my remembrance all things He said to me (John 14:26).

Because the light had turned on for me, I mapped out the Bible in timelines, people, promises, and progressive revelations of Jesus. I suddenly had a next-level ability to comprehend and think out things in context of subject matter. I became a walking topical Bible. Part of me had been waiting for Jesus to resurrect it and call it forward. So, it made great sense to me to go to a prophetic Bible college and graduate at the top of my class.

My grandfather, Papa I called him, privately funded my tuition at his favorite preacher's Bible school in another state—a worldwide recognized evangelical and prophetic powerhouse.

This ministry was as big as a ministry could get in 1987, and I was about to jump neck deep into it.

On day one, I found my dorm, met with my counselors, and introduced myself to what would be my friends for the rest of my life. On day two, I was thrown out never to see any of those people again. It was so painful, I did not mention my horrible experience of Bible college for years and years. Here's the scoop of my terrible scandal.

Train Wreck

On the morning of my first full day of Bible college, I was in the cafeteria eating my first breakfast. I was so excited. It was a surreal experience for me. Suddenly, a professional sounding voice came across the loud speaker, "Troy Allen Brewer from Joshua, Texas. Troy Allen Brewer, please report immediately to the Dean's office."

I knew in my heart what was about to happen. They had recognized my musical genius and were going to ask me to be part of the worship team. I might even lead, I imagined.

Seven minutes later, I was standing in front of the Dean and breathing a little heavy from my quick trot from breakfast.

"Have a seat, Troy," he directed. "How was your first night?"

"The chapel service was amazing," I responded. "The students on campus are so nice. There are people from all over the world—from every race and background. I have never been part of anything like this. It's just incredible, sir."

"Yes," he smiled looking directly at me. "Lots of beautiful testimonies for Jesus." We both agreed and nodded our heads at each other. Then he moved to the other side of the chair and the other high hip he was sitting on. "Troy, let me ask you something."

Oh, boy! I thought. *Here comes the big offer.*

"When you look around and see all these people on this campus from all over the world, did you see any who were excessively overweight?"

It took me a minute to process his question and a moment more to calculate the body mass index of everyone I had encountered.

"Why, no, sir. Now that I think about it, I might be the only fat man on campus."

He didn't laugh like I thought he would. Instead, he said, "You are, Troy, and that's a bad testimony. It's our fault that you were allowed through the entrance process, but these kinds of mistakes are made when we allow for such late applications. I'm afraid you are going to have to take the witness and testimony of your life a lot more seriously before you can represent our alumni and continue your education here."

I was devastated. I was too fat for Bible college. I didn't even know that was possible.

Two hours later, I was calling my grandfather from a pay phone off campus.

"I'm too fat for Bible college, Papa. They said I have to lose fifty pounds before I can come back."

There would be no coming back. Horrified by the shame of such a thing, I didn't say anything to anybody and neither did Papa. They didn't give me a ride home, they didn't reimburse my tuition, they just kicked the fat boy back to Johnson County, Texas.

It was not good.

I came back home and hit the ground running. I picked right back up with my band, went to work as a phone counselor for the 700 Club, and started outreaches to the homeless under the I-45 bridge in Dallas. I never tried to go to college anywhere again.

It hurt me badly, and I was scared to death my friends and family would find out. It's a stigma that haunted me every day and I couldn't tell anybody about it.

Sounds like something that needs redemption, right? Wait until you see what Jesus has done for me from that very moment in time.

Fast Forward

In 2015, I began to think a lot about the shame and the missed opportunity of that event back in 1987. I had been practicing the power of redeeming time for several years now, and I suddenly realized I had never asked Jesus to supernaturally redeem that time.

So, I sat down, broke out a calendar, and got into the presence of the Lord. I confessed the entire situation to King Jesus and repented for the hurt and the shame.

I invited the presence of Jesus into the Dean's office and into the phone booth I called my Papa from. I declared His honor in that place in time was much greater than my shame. I asked the Holy Spirit to show me the presence of the King, and I immediately saw that Jesus felt sorry for the position I was in, and even the position the Dean was in. Jesus hated the whole scenario and He was going to redeem it with the power of His blood.

Enter the Redemptive Dreamer

Despite not completing one day of "higher education," this fat man began getting supernatural promptings from the Lord to start writing books. One of the books I wrote was titled *Numbers that Preach: Understanding God's Mathematical Lingo.* It was all about the numbers in the Bible and how God speaks hidden prophetic messages through them. It's an amazing teaching and something that once you see it, you can't un-see it. Surprisingly, it was a pretty popular book.

In 2016, I was invited to guest host John Paul Jackson's TV show, *Dreams and Mysteries.* I recorded several episodes that caught the attention of prophetic people worldwide.

My friend, Steve Maddox, who produced and directed the show with his wife, Ginny, began to prophesy great words and new direction into my life. They introduced me to people like Jamie Galloway and Rabbi Jason Sobel. It was another shining time for me.

About halfway through the year, a kid from our church had entered into the theology program at Texas Christian University. He called me super excited.

"Did you know your book, *Numbers that Preach,* is required reading for the class I'm in?"

"What!? You are kidding," I chimed back.

It was really remarkable because my biological grandfather had been a history professor at TCU. I was overjoyed and immediately moved it to the front burner of my Kingdom thinking. I started becoming watchful.

A few days later, a prophetic teacher and friend named Sharon Bolen called me and said she had found my book in the school library of Southwest Baptist Theological Seminary. All this in the same week, and I knew this redemption was coming from a different flow of time than what I had previously experienced after Bible school.

I stopped and prayed. I asked the Holy Spirit to let me see more of His redemption and honor in place of my shame from that time frame. While I was praying, a brilliant and wondrous thought came to me. I quickly got on the Internet and looked up the phone number for the school I had been thrown out of 19 years earlier.

I spoke to several people and after some direction, I found the required reading list for students. There it was! My book, *Numbers that Preach* is required reading in the same theological seminary from which I was expelled!

This fat man is instructing the skinny students and bringing them into prophetic encounters of joy. It's listed in their library and noted as "a must-read for anyone interested in prophetic numbers of the Bible." Now that is redemption!

A Prayer of Redeeming a Time of Great Shame into a Time of Great Honor

(Mark the day, name what happened.)

King Jesus I lift to You the day of________________ when ________________ happened. This has been a time of great shame for me and something terrible to even think about. You know exactly what happened and how it happened. You know what was my fault and what wasn't. You also know how terrible this has been and the damage it has done.

I confess my guilt and shame. I confess the detrimental effect it has had on me. I confess the way I handled it then and have handled it since has not been good. I forgive all involved who have hurt me and ask that You forgive me for my part in this, Jesus. I ask You, Lord, to overcome this evil with the goodness of Your honor. Please bring redemption into this place on my timeline.

(Call upon His manifest presence in that terrible place.)

I call upon my Redeemer! I ask You, King Jesus, to be with me in that very moment. I ask You, Lord, that Your will, Your heart, and Your way in that moment of time be done the way it's done in heaven. Be physically, emotionally, mentality, and spiritually with me on that date so many years ago. I invite you to fill up that time and space with Your eternal and manifest presence. Bring redemption, healing, and correction, King Jesus.

(Go after the prophetic gift of seeing and personally encountering (tasting) His presence there in that place.)

> *Oh, taste and see that the LORD is good; blessed is the man who trusts in Him.*
>
> —Psalm 34:8

Holy Spirit, show me the manifest presence of Jesus with me in that place. Give me an eye to see and an ear to hear. Line up my perception with You, Holy Spirit, and cause the scales to fall from my eyes. Give me a heart to know Jesus in that moment for evermore. Open my eyes to see Him there and open my ears to hear His words in that place. Show me the ministry of the Lord in that time and help me glorify the Lord for His presence there.

(Praise and worship King Jesus in this place.)

I praise you my God that your goodness overcomes this evil. Your presence displaces the enemy. Darkness flees at Your light! The bondage of my shame is released at the presence of Your majesty. You have come to set me free and I love You for it. I praise You for Your heart and Your power. I declare that God was with me then, is with me now, and will continue to be with me in the future.

(Prophetically declare and celebrate.)

I declare I have been redeemed and set free from that terrible thief by the blood of the Lamb. I am no longer a slave to shame. The Lord has covered me with righteousness. The God of heaven has vindicated me and calls me honored and favored. Now, let my time change! Let the throne of His presence produce life from that very moment into my right now time, in Jesus' name. Amen.

Be prepared to see, note, and mark the changes that are coming from that redeemed place. Call those things "the precious things of God" and keep them holy. Make a big deal out of every subtle change that will turn into a tool for transformation.

Remember, Elijah proclaimed the drought was over when he saw the first tiny cloud. He supernaturally advanced at an accelerated rate and brought a downpour in the process.

Then it came to pass the seventh time, that he said, "There is a cloud, as small as a man's hand, rising out of the sea!" So, he said, "Go up, say to Ahab, 'Prepare your chariot, and go down before the rain stops you.'" Now it happened in the meantime that the sky became black with clouds and wind, and there was a heavy rain. So, Ahab rode away and went to Jezreel. Then the hand of the Lord came upon Elijah; and he girded up his loins and ran ahead of Ahab to the entrance of Jezreel.

—1 Kings 18:44-46

22

More Places in Time to Redeem and More Testimonies of the Outcome of Redeeming Time

Let me suggest some other places in your timeline that may need redemption. I give you some testimonies as well.

1. Redeeming the times of wasted years or lost investment.

When time is redeemed, nothing is wasted. The Lord of the harvest will cause you to reap in places you have not sown if you have not reaped in the places you have sown. There is still a harvest for you realize. (See Luke 10:2.)

Your investment is not lost once redemption comes in. If your investment was being dedicated to someone for years of your life and they left you anyway, Jesus knows how to redeem that mess.

If your investment was actual money you put into something or someone and you got ripped off, the Lord knows how to redeem that mess.

Leanna and I once made a $60,000 investment into a Christian group of Kingdom investors. We were devastated by a thief and lost everything. Not just us but all of our friends who had invested as well.

Since applying the blood and bringing Kingdom dominion into the time frame, we have seen many $60,000 miracles! The exact amount of money we lost in our investment has returned to us over and over again from nonrelated income streams. Our Redeemer lives!

2. Redeeming a time of great failure.

Whether it's moral failure or failure to accomplish something, redeeming time is perfect for you. You don't run away from Jesus in these places. You actually invite Him into your worst failures and depend upon Him as your Redeemer. One of my favorite testimonies of redeeming time comes in this category.

John was a hardened convict who had spent more than 22 years in a Texas gladiator farm (aka: prison). His face was tattooed and his body marked with graffiti from the gangs he belonged to throughout the years.

Just before his release from prison, John had a true encounter with King Jesus that changed everything. Being back home had not been easy for him and transition into society was nearly impossible because of his history and his physical appearance.

"I can't find a job, Pastor Troy. Nobody will hire me because of my tats. I don't blame 'em," he said, starting to sink into hopelessness.

After being out for more than a year, the only work he could find was temporary day jobs. He needed a real job—but what he really needed was to redeem his time.

You already know what we did. I asked him if he could remember the day his sentence was announced and the judge found him guilty.

"Worst day of my life," he said in a heavy Hispanic accent. "I knew everything my old man said about me was going to be true. I knew my wife would leave me and my kids were going to grow up without me."

We invited King Jesus to invade that space in time, that courtroom 23 years ago. We invited the Lord to stand with him during the sentencing and the verdict. We asked Jesus to forgive him of the selfish crimes he had committed against other people. We asked the Lord to bring redemption and for the heart of the Redeemer to rule and reign instead of the enemy. We pronounced an end to the curse and we celebrated the presence of the Lord.

The Very Next Day

That was on a Sunday night. On Monday morning, John woke up thinking about a company he had never had the courage to apply for a job at because he had heard they did not hire convicted felons.

Nonetheless, John believed it was God, so about two hours later, he began the daunting task of filling out an application. Struggling to make his writing look good and his information look promising, the boss noticed him and asked him to step out to talk.

"What kind of job are you looking for?" he asked.

"I'm pretty good at welding and I have my license. I can do other stuff too, but I'm good at welding," John answered.

"OK. Come on back." And just like that he was given a hood for his head, gloves, and a welding job for the rest of the day as a tryout.

At the end of the day, the boss told him he was ready to hire him, but he had to finish the application process. Being kind-hearted, he knew John couldn't read or write very well, he filled out the application for him while asking John questions.

"Are you a convicted felon?" he asked.

"Yes, sir. I am. I did 22 years for robbery, possession of a gun, and getting caught with a carload of dope. I was eighteen years old and I've been out now for a full year without any trouble."

"OK," he said, looking up from his glasses. "I thought you might be and the policy of our company is not to hire people convicted of a felony. Still, I'm going to process your paperwork, get your prison record, talk to your probation officer, and send in a recommendation to hire you anyway."

"Oh, man! That would be great, sir," he said with hope.

"I'll run it through slowly, and it might take a couple of weeks. In the meantime, you can work for me until they tell me you can't be hired. Will you do a good job for me, John?"

"Yes, sir. I will," John said.

"If it comes back and I have to fire you, I know some guys who might hire you. I'm going to test drive your work ethic and ability to work with others while you are still with me. I don't like to recommend people I have not vetted."

"Yes, sir. I understand. Thank you, sir," John said.

To John's amazement, the boss stood up and said, "You'll work for me starting tomorrow morning. The pay is $22 an hour and you have a ten-hour day."

My friend was instantly making $220 a day after serving 22 years in prison. The number 22 is all about the light of God being made manifest in our lives and that's what happened for my friend. Now that is redemption!

That was almost three years ago and, as far as I know, John still works for that same man and that same company. He did get hired after all, and do you know why? When they ran his criminal history, they couldn't find any record of his crime or imprisonment. He assured them he had done the crime and the time. They ran it through again, and even one more time, before deciding not to try any longer.

The day after we invited Jesus to redeem his time, John's record of crime and punishment had disappeared. Our Redeemer lives!

> *He has not dealt with us according to our sins,*
> *Nor punished us according to our iniquities.*
> *For as the heavens are high above the earth,*
> *So great is His mercy toward those who fear Him;*

As far as the east is from the west,
So far has He removed our transgressions from us.
As a father pities his children,
So, the Lord pities those who fear Him.
For He knows our frame; [our time frame too]
He remembers that we are dust.

—Psalm 103:10-14

3. Redeeming a time of bondage.

Invite the Lord into any time or season of your life you were owned by something or someone—a terrible relationship, an addiction, a situation of poverty, or abuse. Many of us need to bring redemption to years we were under the bondage of religious ideas and practices.

4. Redeeming a time of great injustice.

This is where you have been accused of something you did not do. Any time you can find a great injustice has come to you that pronounced something terribly wrong into your life, that's where you should bring redemption. The Lord is your vindication!

I once had trouble with a church board that nearly killed me. I mean my actual life, not to mention my ministry, and all I have devoted my life to. I weighed about 400 pounds and it's a miracle I didn't have a stroke or heart attack during this time of great anguish. Don't worry, I lost 160 pounds in 2012. Let me tell you the story and how God has redeemed it.

First, let me take you back in time. I love the history of entertainment and my story of the big church split reminds me of Orson Wells.

War of the Worlds

They didn't know it would cause a panic. Orson Wells sat at a press conference seemingly stunned, excited, and thrilled at the marketing opportunity of a room full of reporters. I don't think he cared that they were demanding answers to allegations of causing hysteria and chaos.

It was Sunday, October 30, and in 1938, CBS was not a TV network. In that time, people saw the world through the sounds of the radio. The day before Halloween, the Mercury Theatre produced a show adapted from H.G. Wells and intended it to be a horror/sci-fi story. They wanted it to seem real and to be scary. It was.

Seventy-three years later in 2011, my beautiful wife and I sat at a church board meeting, opposite family, friends, and ministry partners whom we had trusted with the finances of the church just a few months earlier.

Just like Orson Wells' press conference, we were in a room full of hateful people with terrible accusations demanding immediate compliance.

Unlike Orson Wells, we were not amused or even strong. We literally cried, sobbed, and begged as they vowed to "shut us down," "kick us out," and "tell the whole world we were stealing." It wasn't just a disagreement. It was way worse than that. A Jezebel manipulator who had tremendous influence on the weak-minded men of my board, had thrown a fit and worked her magic in a very successful way.

It was a war between worlds and my front-row seat to how ugly it is when godly people don't understand the Kingdom. It changed me forever.

The accusation of stealing came from a destroying spirit she was in league with.

"When you take money from Joshua, Texas, and spend it on people who live in Africa, that's stealing," she said.

"Yes, yes," the board agreed like puppets.

Now, to Kingdom Christians, that's called missions. We had been doing radical missions, including funding major orphanages and leper ministries, for fifteen years and now they wanted to stop it if she couldn't control it.

"When you take money that comes from a church congregation and spend it on tens of thousands of people who will never go to our church, that's mishandling the money," she said.

No. That's called feeding the poor through the OpenDoor Food Bank. We give away more than six million pounds of food every year to people who might never go to our church. We don't do this to get people to come to church. We do this because we *are* the Church. I had never imagined people on my team would object to this, but it turns out they were not on my team.

"When you mortgage your own house to pay for orphanages in India and Uganda, that's incompetence," they concurred.

No. That's called selling out for the hidden treasure in the field God has trusted you with. We have always been radical in our dedication to our calling. They should have been proud of us, but to them, it was proof we were irresponsible idiots.

I had made the biggest mistake of my life. Unwilling to be a leader and handle the church finances, I had personally handpicked a church board that I thought I could trust. I was afraid I wasn't smart enough to handle the money and handed a piece of my calling over to people I loved. Now, after just a few months of power, here we were defending how we had done ministry for more than 15 years—a big lesson in leadership for me.

We sat in disbelief as they told us we were not allowed to do missions or the food bank any longer. All this "in the name of responsibility and accountability," she said. Nothing in the name of Jesus.

What she wanted was control over all the money, and I had answered her the way Travis answered Santa Anna at the Alamo. I fired her. The board, her friends, and family, would not have it. They demanded I actually work for her and have her run all my ministries.

She was not on the board, but she had great influence with some of the biggest personalities. She swayed them with her drama the way Orson Wells convinced New Jersey that intergalactic monsters had landed at Grover's Mill.

Meanwhile, I ran around like a wandering puppy dog just hoping nobody would kick. I was inexperienced and totally out of my league with how to handle these guys. I didn't know what to do or say and none of it was ever right. I was a mess and clueless on how to lead and be confident in the solid front they mounted against me.

Lickety Split

In the weeks that followed, our church "grew" from over 800 people to less than 100 people. In the sixteenth year of the ministry Leanna and I founded, we needed someone like the sixteenth president to deal with our very uncivil war. I don't think Lincoln would have signed up for our mess.

Instead of fruitful harvests, we saw nothing but burning fields, and it was an extremely painful season.

I will never allow myself to forget how damaging and detrimental this event was to everything God was doing in us and through us. After this, I learned how to be a leader, how to give the left foot of fellowship, and how to truly be successful, but it wasn't a happy learning experience.

We survived. We even overcame it, but at great, great cost on every gauge on my smashed up dashboard.

The night of the big church split and Gong Show board meeting was June 14, 2011. I will never forget it.

The last thing one of the most colorful performers said to me was, "Troy, in three months, your church will be dead with chains on the door. Your ministry is going to be over and you are going to be homeless. Don't come looking to me for a job or a place to stay."

Oh, it was terrible. The biggest cry the enemy spoke to our mediator was, "We are never going to have a nice building. We are never going to have anything nice. Troy just gives it all away to nonchurch people and it just isn't right."

Back to the Future

Fast-forward two years to the day—the very day. On June 14, 2013, I was sitting in the office of a well-known preacher in our region. I had been invited the day before and now I was wondering what this meeting was all about.

We had never done ministry together. We knew of each other and respected each other, but I had never preached at her church or she at mine.

"The Lord told me to do it like this," she said. "Hold out your hands." I held them both out like a cup and she dropped a big set of keys into them.

"Troy, the Lord told me to invite you here, give you every building I own, and merge my church with your church," said Pastor Gloria Gillaspie of Lighthouse Church in Burleson, Texas.

Today, the multimillion dollar OpenDoor Church campus is home to thousands of people each week. That big beautiful church building, all the adjacent buildings, and property were given to me. All of it and on the very date of the horrible injustice pronounced against me and my wife.

"We will never have a nice building," was said because of the money we spent on missions and outreach.

"Here's a 5.7 million dollar campus," Pastor Gloria said because the Lord told her He was going to reward us for how we selflessly serve people all around the world.

I know I mentioned the exact date and how it was the same. This happens when you redeem your time. *The time markers for great loss become time markers for great reward.*

Did you catch what day June 14 is? It's Flag Day—Jehovah Nissi—The Lord is my Banner. This name for God is found in Exodus 17:15. When the Lord is your banner, He is the game-changing Redeemer who brings a different momentum onto your battlefield.

I know what I am talking about. Redeeming time is real.

God will right your wrongs and bring vindication. No need to have unforgiveness or form your own mob. Our Redeemer lives!

I encourage you to make a mental note of at least three more places that might need redeeming time.

5. Redeeming times when you were absent for people you should have been there for and vice versa.

6. Redeeming times of lost opportunity.

This is when you could have done something amazing but went AWOL instead.

I remember in 1986 I had an opportunity to buy 70 acres of land in Hill County, Texas. I looked at it and spoke with the man who owned it. I was a newly saved teenager and totally green. I had no idea what I was going to do with 70 acres, but the man selling it really liked me and wanted me to have it.

Add to that, I had a dream. In this dream, a pastor friend of mine was driving a tractor and plowing up a field. Hundreds and hundreds of gold coins were in his wake. While it was a cool dream, I didn't know what it meant. I was very young.

I felt a real urgency from the Holy Spirit that this was an amazing opportunity God had for me. I heard God tell me to buy that land. It was cheap, but $45,000 seemed like $10 million to me back then. I let my fear and some bad counsel from people who told me I wasn't smart enough and "had no business buying land" get the best of me. I let that land go.

Several years later, I ran into that man and he asked what I was doing with my life. Was I a Christian rock legend? Was I a world-famous pastor? No, I told him. I was a pastor with a tiny church and a big family, barely making ends meet. Heck, my wife and I were so poor, we didn't even have electricity or glass in many of the windows.

"I'm sorry to hear that," the man told me. So was I, but what I heard next made me not only sorry, but mad. That 70 acres was the first and richest natural gas field in our part of Texas. A few years after somebody else bought that 70 acres, the new technology of horizontal drilling began in north Texas on that very property. The person who owned it had a ridiculous number of zeroes in their bank account and it could have been mine. It was supposed to be mine.

That tore me up for a very long time. I felt stupid. I felt betrayed. Years later, I understood redeeming time and this was a moment in time I took the Lord back to. I asked Him to redeem that time and that place. I asked for and gave forgiveness. I was thankful to the Lord for all He gave me despite my not trusting Him during that time.

Guess what? Just after I prayed that, crazy land deals started coming my way. I bought a 47,000 square foot multimillion-dollar church facility for a mere few hundred thousand dollars. A man gave me five acres in rural Joshua where I built the OpenDoor Food Bank. My wife and I bought our dream ranch for half its appraised value.

Pastor Gloria followed the Lord's leading and merged our churches, giving me an even bigger, more beautiful facility. That same month, I was given an acre of land in India to build an orphanage, feeding ministry, and leper home. One acre doesn't sound like much, but in this part of India, land is $1 million per acre. That's six zeroes! In just under four weeks, I had million-dollar properties on both sides of the pond—literally, 12 hours apart as American Airlines flies—given to me.

That's restoration, redemption, and maybe even a little restitution! When the Word says the Lord removes our sins as far as the east is from the west (Psalm 103:12), He also does that with our shame and pain. Isn't He just so good?

7. Redeeming the time of family in times way past.

My friend Will Ford III is a world-changing Jesus freak. If you don't know who I'm talking about, you need to look him up. Many know him internationally, however, for a family heirloom passed down through history, and its connection to slavery and prayer for freedom.

He has a cast iron cooking kettle that belonged to his ancestors, who were slaves in Louisiana over 150 years ago. His people were not allowed to pray for freedom so they would turn the kettle over, put some small rocks under the rim, and whisper their prayer for freedom into that kettle.

They prayed for the release of their children from slavery. Remarkably, Will now leads a national prayer movement on the release of racial hatred and injustice.

As a leader in this prayer movement, Will uses this "prayer bowl" (Revelation 5:8) as a catalyst for mobilizing prayer and teaching on intercession, revival, and societal transformation. It's crazy cool! Redemption has caused him to be the fulfillment of those prayers his ancestors prayed.

He believes that it was the prayers of a godly remnant of all races—revivalists and abolitionists—that brought revival to America and ultimately ended slavery. Receiving their mantle from yesterday, Will is actively training a new generation to release justice to the most marginalized today.

To top that off, he is now best friends and ministry partners with a man named Matt Lockett. After years of working and living life together, they found out Matt's family had owned Will's family. Dr. Martin Luther King Jr. said in his famous "I Have a Dream" speech: "I have a dream that one day on the red hills of Georgia the sons of former slaves and the sons of former slave-owners will be able to sit down together at a table of brotherhood."

Will and Matt are the fulfillment of that dream and those prayers. Their timelines and that of their ancestors were redeemed and these men are now sitting at the table of brotherhood, racial justice, and healing.

Do you see how you can redeem the time and prayers of our ancestors to bring fulfillment of the promises God gave them, but into our lives right now? I'm telling you, redemption is God's highest priority.

I am also telling you that the blood of Jesus is the physical matter that overcomes all time, space, and matter.

23

The Practice of Past Redemption, Present Redemption, and Future Redemption

As already stated, it's a fact that when God created time, He created past, present, and future time all at once.

Mostly when I think about time and redemption, I think about past time and present time. I have spent an entire book speaking on the powerful reality of redeeming time past but make sure you know how to redeem the present time.

Bringing the King's redemption into your "right now" time is all about connecting with His manifest presence in every moment. Even in the places where He is hidden throughout your day, He is with you. Jesus is just as present when He is hidden as when He is clearly seen.

> *...and lo, I am with you always, even to the end of the age.*
>
> —Matthew 28:20

Even if you can't detect the hand of God, you can always go after the heart of God:

> *...The Lord hath sought him a man after his own heart, and the Lord hath commanded him to be captain over his people....*
>
> —1 Samuel 13:14 KJV

Learning to live a life of full disclosure before God and saying, "Here I am. All of me," is how you bring redemption into every "right now." Recommitting your life to be available to God's presence is everything when it comes to redeeming present time.

Redeeming Future Time

I bet you have already done this, even if you don't know it.

"Lord, be with me tomorrow in court," or "God, please help me in that job interview." These are simple examples of asking God to meet you in the future—to bring His presence into your timeline that is future tense to you, but not to God.

I think that when you ask God to meet you in the future, a day or two, or several decades from now, He actually steps into that place right then. All time is present time to God. He doesn't have a past or future.

"I Am"

He is present tense. He immediately steps into that place knowing you will get there later for you, but now for Him. There is the passing of time for you, but not for Him. He steps in and out of time the way He steps in and out of rooms with doors that are shut (see John 20:19).

So, there is nothing wrong with you praising Him for being there now.

I have listed a couple of wild possibilities for you to consider in redeeming future time.

Ask Jesus to visit you on your last day and to make your last minutes glorify Him. You don't have to wait for that day to ask Him to be there (see John 21:19). You don't have to worry if you will finish well or if you will be freaked out. Ask Him to meet you, in the future for you but right now for Him, in your final moments. Worship Him and thank Him for His presence, and for the fragrance of heaven to be evident to everyone around you.

Ask Jesus to meet you there and ask Him to show you what that looks like.

> *LORD, make me to know my end, and what is the measure of my days, that I may know how frail I am.*
>
> —Psalm 39:4

Not only is it biblical to ask Jesus to show you what your end looks like, you can ask Him how many days you have left.

My father-in-law, Ray Knight, told me that the Lord has visited him a year and half before his death. He told me what Jesus told him, "I'll be here this Christmas and the next Christmas, but I'll be with Him," he said pointing up, "before the next New Year's."

Ray died the day after Christmas the following year. He called the shots because the Lord was already with him on that day. He wasn't afraid. He finished very well because God met him there.

Ray's grandfather had actually prophesied to the day when he would be with the Lord. After putting the last nail in a church he had spent more than a year building, and prophesying that his funeral would be the very first service in that church, he went home. He put on the suit he wanted to be buried in, called his son and told him he loved him, then got in bed, suit on, and died comfortably.

The Holman Christian Standard Bible translates Psalm 39:4 like this:

> *LORD, reveal to me the end of my life and the number of my days. Let me know how short-lived I am.*

The International Standard Version puts it this way:

> *LORD, let me know how my life ends, and the standard by which you will measure my days, whatever it is! Then I will know how transient my life is.*

You are not going to be afraid because He is with you. You will not be full of terror because He is your peace.

> *Mark the perfect man, and behold the upright: for the end of that man is peace.*
>
> —Psalm 37:37 KJV

As a matter of fact, you don't have to wait for any bad thing to happen to ask Jesus to show up and take over in any future date. If you need His redemption, ask Him now.

Are you afraid of getting old? Ask God to redeem that time for you.

Are you afraid of the time when your children are getting married or moving out? Ask God to be with you then and bring His redemption.

You no longer have to be chained to anything in your future. There's no scenario you can imagine in your timeline that you do not have the ability and responsibility to bring the Kingdom and the blood of the Lamb into.

A Prayer for Redeeming Time Future

King Jesus, You call me toward my destiny. You deal with me in future present tense. You know my days, when I rise up and when I fall down. Please meet me in every epic moment. Cause me to know Your presence and to find You there. Show me things that I don't know how to handle before I get to those places, and make me victorious there.

You are the wielder of time and I ask You, God, to conform my future timelines to glorify You. Work all things for my good. Make me victorious and cause me to finish well.

Meet me on the day I die and tell me how much time I have between now and then. Show me what my last day looks like, where You are with me, how You are with me, and what You are ministering to me. I praise You for being in that place! I worship You for not leaving me alone in any hour. My time belongs to you. I am headed toward You in my future, and surely goodness and mercy will follow me there. I love You, Sir! Amen!

24

In Conclusion

When God created all things and joined His creation to time, space, and matter, He programmed its DNA with components of hope that cannot be altered.

Anyone can access hope to all things past, present, and future because anyone can access Jesus in any way they perceive time. It's all part of the beauty and genius of God.

The sweet redemption of King Jesus is meant to be discovered and experienced without measure. Our key to the power of this beautiful marriage between the Lord and His bride is simply never being able to imagine any part of our lives without first thinking about our life with Him.

That's the key to any beautiful marriage.

So, in wrapping this up, let me remind you that you still have time. Your past time is still your past time and Jesus wants you to discover Him and experience Him there. Your present time is your time with Him to live and breathe His life more abundantly. Your future time is ready to be the room where Jesus is unveiling His glory in new prophetic upgrades and green lights of joyous discovery and adventure.

Jesus is thrilled at the opportunity to live life with you in the dangerous places of time, space, and matter. His heart longs to find us thrilled at the same opportunity to live with Him in those same places.

When we find Him there, we find He is not afraid. He is victorious and full of hope. He is full of appreciation and love of life. He is willing and ready to confront evil, and bless every place with transformation and His Kingdom dominion.

He wants to find us in those same places exactly like He is. He wants to make us be as He is because we see Him instead of seeing our slave master in time.

The promise of the Word is that when we see Him, we will be like Him. Now that is redeeming time.

> *...but we know that when He is revealed, we shall be like Him, for we shall see Him as He is.*
>
> —1 John 3:2

Hope for every time and season. A cross for every time and season. Redemption and exchange of life for death for every hour of every day.

So, now it is time to accept the invitation, permission, and commandment to change your measures of time to places where King Jesus rules from His throne. He wants to bring His Kingdom and save you in every way a person can be saved.

Our Redeemer lives and is not subject to time. Time is made subject to Him. Redeeming time says the salvation of your past, present, and future is not behind you or in front of you. The Great I AM is ready to bring your redemption and salvation to all things past, present, and future. He is ready right now.

> *For He says: "In an acceptable time I have heard you, and in the day of salvation I have helped you." Behold, now is the accepted time; behold, now is the day of salvation.*
>
> —2 Corinthians 6:2

Peace to you!

Section Six

SCRIPTURES FOR REDEEMING TIME

Time

In the beginning (time) God created the heavens (space) and the earth (matter).

> *Then God said, "Let there be light": and there was light. And God saw the light, that it was good; and God divided the light from the darkness. God called the light Day, and the darkness He called Night. So the evening and the morning were the first day.*
>
> —Genesis 1:3-5

Daniel knew God as "Ancient of Days" which means "older than time." He calls God "Ancient of Days" three times in Daniel chapter 7.

> *I watched till thrones were put in place, and the Ancient of Days was seated; His garment was white*

> *as snow, and the hair of His head was like pure wool. His throne was a fiery flame, its wheels a burning fire.*
>
> —Daniel 7:9

God told Moses His very name was synonymous with eternity.

> *And God said unto Moses, I Am That I Am: and he said, Thus shalt thou say unto the children of Israel, I Am hath sent me unto you. And God said moreover unto Moses, Thus shalt thou say unto the children of Israel, the Lord God of your fathers, the God of Abraham, the God of Isaac, and the God of Jacob, hath sent me unto you: this is my name for ever, and this is my memorial unto all generations.*
>
> —Exodus 3:14-15 KJV

> *And He is before all things, and in Him all things consist.* (NIV says, *He is before all things, and in him all things hold together.)*
>
> —Colossians 1:17

> *My times are in Your hand; deliver me from the hand of my enemies, and from those who persecute me.*
>
> —Psalm 31:15

> *Ah, Lord God! Behold, You have made the heavens and the earth by Your great power and outstretched arm. There is nothing too hard for You.*
>
> —Jeremiah 32:17

For God is not the author of confusion but of peace, as in all the churches of the saints.

—1 Corinthians 14:33

Now when they came up out of the water, the Spirit of the Lord caught Philip away, so that the eunuch saw him no more; and he went on his way rejoicing. But Philip was found at Azotus....

—Acts 8:39-40

For a thousand years in Your sight are like yesterday when it is past, and like a watch in the night.

—Psalm 90:4

But, beloved, do not forget this one thing, that with the Lord one day is as a thousand years, and a thousand years as one day.

—2 Peter 3:8

So the Lord God said to the serpent: "Because you have done this, you are cursed more than all cattle, and more than every beast of the field; on your belly you shall go, and you shall eat dust all the days of your life. And I will put enmity between you and the woman, and between your seed and her Seed; He shall bruise your head, and you shall bruise His heel."

—Genesis 3:14-15

As far as the east is from the west, so far has He removed our transgressions from us.

—Psalm 103:12

"I am the Alpha and the Omega, the Beginning and the End," says the Lord, "who is and who was and who is to come, the Almighty."

—Revelation 1:8

So I will restore to you the years that the swarming locust has eaten, the crawling locust, the consuming locust, and the chewing locust, My great army which I sent among you.

—Joel 2:25

And we know that all things work together for good to those who love God, to those who are the called according to His purpose.

—Romans 8:28

And by Him to reconcile all things to Himself, by Him, whether things on earth or things in heaven, having made peace through the blood of His cross.

—Colossians 1:20

Then God said, "Let there be lights in the firmament of the heavens to divide the day from the night; and let them be for signs and seasons, and for days and years; and let them be for lights in the firmament of the heavens to give light on the earth"; and it was so. Then God made two great lights: the greater light to rule the day, and the lesser light to rule the night. He made the stars also. God set them in the firmament of the heavens to give light on the earth, and to rule over the day and over the night, and to divide the light from the darkness. And God saw that it was good.

—Genesis 1:14-18

To everything there is a season, a time for every purpose under heaven:
A time to be born, and a time to die;
A time to plant, and a time to pluck what is planted;
A time to kill, and a time to heal;
A time to break down, and a time to build up;
A time to weep, and a time to laugh;
A time to mourn, and a time to dance;
A time to cast away stones, and a time to gather stones;
A time to embrace, and a time to refrain from embracing;
A time to gain, and a time to lose;
A time to keep, and a time to throw away;
A time to tear, and a time to sew;
A time to keep silence, and a time to speak;
A time to love, and a time to hate;
A time of war, and a time of peace.

—Ecclesiastes 3:1-8

While the earth remains, seedtime and harvest, cold and heat, summer and winter, and day and night shall not cease.

—Genesis 8:22

And the children of Issachar, which were men that had understanding of the times, to know what Israel ought to do; the heads of them were two hundred; and all their brethren were at their command.

—1 Chronicles 12:32

Go to the ant, you sluggard; consider its ways and be wise! It has no commander, no overseer or ruler, yet it gathers its provisions in summer and gathers its food at harvest.

—Proverbs 6:6-8 NIV

In the morning you shall say, "Oh, that it were evening!" And at evening you shall say, "Oh, that it were morning!" because of the fear which terrifies your heart, and because of the sight which your eyes see.

—Deuteronomy 28:67

In the beginning was the Word, and the Word was with God, and the Word was God. He was in the beginning with God. All things were made through Him, and without Him nothing was made that was made. ...And the Word became flesh and dwelt among us, and we beheld His glory, the glory as of the only begotten of the Father, full of grace and truth.

—John 1:1-3,14

So the sun stood still, and the moon stopped, till the nation avenged itself on its enemies, as it is written in the Book of Jasher. The sun stopped in the middle of the sky and delayed going down about a full day.

—Joshua 10:13 NIV

...the plowman shall overtake the reaper....

—Amos 9:13

I will make the shadow cast by the sun go back the ten steps it has gone down on the stairway of Ahaz....

—Isaiah 38:8 NIV

Come now, and let us reason together," says the Lord, "Though your sins are like scarlet, they shall be as white as snow; though they are red like crimson, they shall be as wool."

—Isaiah 1:18

To console those who mourn in Zion, to give them beauty for ashes, the oil of joy for mourning, the garment of praise for the spirit of heaviness; that they may be called trees of righteousness, the planting of the Lord, that He may be glorified.

—Isaiah 61:3

So I will restore to you the years that the swarming locust has eaten....

—Joel 2:25

Redeeming the time, because the days are evil.

—Ephesians 5:16

Walk in wisdom toward those who are outsiders, redeeming the time.

—Colossians 4:5

The king answered and said, "I know for certain that you would gain time, because you see that my decision is firm."

—Daniel 2:8

So teach us to number our days, that we may apply our hearts unto wisdom.

—Psalm 90:12 KJV

Remember now your Creator in the days of your youth, before the difficult days come and the years draw near when you say, "I have no pleasure in them."

—Ecclesiastes 12:1

And we know that all things work together for good [redeeming time] *to those who love God, to those who are called according to His purpose. For whom He foreknew, He also predestined to be conformed to the image of His Son, that He might be the firstborn among many brethren. Moreover whom He predestined, these He also called; whom He called, these He also justified; and whom He justified, these He also glorified.*

—Romans 8:28-30

But this I say, brethren, the time is short: it remaineth, that both they that have wives be as though they had none.

—1 Corinthians 7:29 KJV

And they that use this world, as not abusing it: for the fashion of this world passeth away.

—1 Corinthians 7:31 KJV

See then that you walk carefully, not as fools, but as wise.

—Ephesians 5:15

"I am the Alpha and the Omega, the Beginning and the End," says the Lord, "who is and who was and who is to come, the Almighty."

—Revelation 1:8

Times and Seasons

Then God said, "Let there be lights in the firmament of the heavens to divide the day from the night; and let them be for signs and seasons, and for days and years; and let them be for lights in the firmament of the heavens to give light on the earth"; and it was so. Then God made two great lights: the greater light to rule the day, and the lesser light to rule the night. He made the stars also. God set them in the firmament of the heavens to give light on the earth, and to rule over the day and over the night, and to divide the light from the darkness. And God saw that it was good.

—Genesis 1:14-18

While the earth remains, seedtime and harvest, cold and heat, winter and summer, and day and night shall not cease.

—Genesis 8:22

He shall be like a tree planted by the rivers of water, that brings forth its fruit in its season, whose leaf also shall not wither; and whatever he does shall prosper.

—Psalm 1:3

He appointed the moon for seasons; the sun knows its going down.

—Psalm 104:19

He has made everything beautiful in its time. Also He has put eternity in their hearts, except that no one can find out the work that God does from beginning to end.

—Ecclesiastes 3:11

For as the rain comes down, and the snow from heaven, and do not return there, but water the earth, And make it bring forth and bud, that it may give seed to the sower and bread to the eater, so shall My word be that goes forth from My mouth; it shall not return to Me void, but it shall accomplish what I please, and it shall prosper in the thing for which I sent it.

—Isaiah 55:10-11

And He changes the times and the seasons; He removes kings and raises up kings; He gives wisdom to the wise and knowledge to those who have understanding.

—Daniel 2:21

And He said to them, "It is not for you to know times or seasons which the Father has put in His own authority."

—Acts 1:7

Do not be deceived, God is not mocked; for whatever a man sows, that he will also reap. For he who sows to his flesh will of the flesh reap corruption, but he who sows to the Spirit will of the Spirit reap everlasting life. And let us not grow weary while doing good, for in due season we shall reap if we do not lose heart. Therefore, as we have opportunity, let us do good to all, especially to those who are of the household of faith.

—Galatians 6:7-10

But concerning the times and the seasons, brethren, you have no need that I should write to you.

—1 Thessalonians 5:1

Eternity and Eternal Life

The Psalms call the place God dwells "everlasting."

Before the mountains were brought forth, or ever You had formed the earth and the world, even from everlasting to everlasting, You are God.

—Psalm 90:2

Eternity—God inhabits

But you, Bethlehem Ephrathah, though you are little among the thousands of Judah, yet out of you shall come forth to Me the One to be Ruler in Israel, whose goings forth are from of old, from everlasting.

—MICAH 5:2

For thus says the high and lofty One who inhabits eternity, whose name is Holy: "I dwell in the high and holy place, with him who has a contrite and humble spirit, to revive the spirit of the humble, and to revive the heart of the contrite ones."

—ISAIAH 57:15

Eternity—God rules

But the LORD is the true God; He is the living God and an everlasting King. At His wrath the earth will tremble, and the nations will not be able to endure His indignation.

—JEREMIAH 10:10

In hope of eternal life which God, who cannot lie, promised before time began.

—TITUS 1:2

And this is the promise that He has promised us—eternal life.

—1 JOHN 2:25

And this is eternal life, that they may know You, the only true God, and Jesus Christ, whom You have sent.

—JOHN 17:3

Who shall not receive manifold more in this present time, and in the world to come life everlasting.

—Luke 18:30 KJV

Then Simon Peter answered him, Lord, to whom shall we go? You have the words of eternal life.

—John 6:68 KJV

Now unto the King eternal, immortal, invisible, the only wise God, be honour and glory forever and ever. Amen.

—1 Timothy 1:17 KJV

I was set up from everlasting, from the beginning, or ever the earth was.

—Proverbs 8:23 KJV

For so an entrance shall be supplied to you abundantly into the everlasting kingdom of our Lord and Savior Jesus Christ.

—2 Peter 1:11

Verily, verily, I say unto you, He that hears my word, and believes on him that sent me, has everlasting life, and shall not come into condemnation; but is passed from death unto life.

—John 5:24 KJV

While we look not at the things which are seen, but at the things which are not seen: for the things which are seen are temporal; but the things which are not seen are eternal.

—2 Corinthians 4:18 KJV

These things have I written unto you that believe on the name of the Son of God; that ye may know that ye have eternal life, and that you may believe on the name of the Son of God.

—1 John 5:13 KJV

But Israel shall be saved in the LORD with an everlasting salvation: ye shall not be ashamed nor confounded world without end.

—Isaiah 45:17 KJV

That whosoever believes in Him should not perish, but have eternal life.

—John 3:15

He has made everything beautiful in its time. Also He has put eternity in their hearts, except that no one can find out the work that God does from the beginning to end.

—Ecclesiastes 3:11

Forever, O LORD, Your word is settled in heaven.

—Psalm 119:89

And these shall go away into everlasting punishment: but the righteous into life eternal.

—Matthew 25:46 KJV

Search the scriptures; for in them ye think ye have eternal life: and they are they which testify of me.

—John 5:39 KJV

Who shall be punished with everlasting destruction from the presence of the Lord, and from the glory of his power.

—2 Thessalonians 1:9 KJV

And we know that the Son of God has come and has given us an understanding, that we may know Him who is true; and we are in Him who is true, even in His Son Jesus Christ. This is the true God and eternal life.

—1 John 5:20

And this is the will of Him who sent me, that everyone who sees the Son and believes in Him may have everlasting life; and I will raise him up at the last day.

—John 6:40

For we know that if our earthly house of this tabernacle were dissolved, we have a building of God, a house not made with hands, eternal in the heavens.

—2 Corinthians 5:1 KJV

For God so loved the world, that he gave his only begotten Son, that whosoever believeth in him should not perish, but have everlasting life.

—John 3:16 KJV

He who has the Son has life; he who does not have the Son of God does not have life.

—1 John 5:12

And this is the testimony: that God has given us eternal life, and this life is in His Son.

—1 John 5:11

Keep yourselves in the love of God, looking for the mercy of our Lord Jesus Christ unto eternal life.

—Jude 1:21

And I know that His command is everlasting life. Therefore, whatever I speak, just as the Father has told Me, so I speak.

—John 12:50

For the life was manifested, and we have seen it, and bear witness, and shew unto you that eternal life, which was with the Father, and was manifested unto us.

—1 John 1:2 KJV

Fight the good fight of faith, lay hold on eternal life, to which thou art also called, and hast professed a good profession before many witnesses.

—1 Timothy 6:12

"But the word of the Lord endures forever." Now this is the word which by the gospel was preached to you.

—Peter 1:25

But whoever drinks of the water that I shall give him shall never thirst. But the water that I shall give him will become in him a fountain of water springing up into everlasting life.

—John 4:14

For this God is our God for ever and ever: he will be our guide even unto death.

—Psalm 48:14 KJV

But grow in grace, and in the knowledge of our Lord and Saviour Jesus Christ. To him be glory both now and for ever. Amen.

—2 Peter 3:18 KJV

That being justified by his grace, we should be made heirs according to the hope of eternal life.

—Titus 3:7 KJV

Do not labor for the food which perishes, but for that food which endures to everlasting life, which the Son of Man will give you, because God the Father has set His seal on Him.

—John 6:27

For the wages of sin is death, but the gift of God is eternal life in Christ Jesus our Lord.

—Romans 6:23

And he who reaps receives wages, and gathers fruit for eternal life, that both he who sows and he who reaps may rejoice together.

—John 4:36

But these are written that you may believe that Jesus is the Christ, the Son of God, and that believing you may have life in His name.

—John 20:31

Kairos—Perfecting Timing

Kairos was translated as "beautiful" in the King James version of the Bible. Its better meaning is "perfect timing."

> *He has made everything beautiful in its time. Also He has put eternity in their hearts, except that no one can find out the work that God does from beginning to end.*
>
> —Ecclesiastes 3:11

> *Now Peter and John went up together to the temple at the hour of prayer, the ninth hour. And a certain man lame from his mother's womb was carried, whom they laid daily at the gate of the temple which is called Beautiful, to ask alms from those who entered the temple; who, seeing Peter and John about to go into the temple, asked for alms. And fixing his eyes on him, with John, Peter said, "Look at us." So he gave them his attention, expecting to receive something from them. Then Peter said, "Silver and gold I do not have, but what I do have I give you: In the name of Jesus Christ of Nazareth, rise up and walk." And he took him by the right hand and lifted him up, and immediately his feet and ankle bones received strength. So he, leaping up, stood and walked and entered the temple with them—walking, leaping, and praising God. And all the people saw him walking and praising God. Then they knew that it was he who sat begging alms at the Beautiful*

Gate of the temple; and they were filled with wonder and amazement at what had happened to him.

—Acts 3:1-10

Searching and Seeking the Times of Your Life—Judging Yourself

Delight yourself also in the Lord, and He shall give you the desires of your heart. Commit your way to the Lord, trust also in Him, and He shall bring it to pass.

—Psalm 37:4-5

You are so intimately aware of me, Lord. You read my heart like an open book and you know all the words I'm about to speak before I even start a sentence! You know every step I will take before my journey even begins. You've gone into the future to prepare the way, and in kindness you follow behind me to spare me from the hurt of my past. With your hand of love upon my life, you impart a blessing to me.

—Psalm 139:3-5 TPT

Where could I go from your Spirit? Where could I run and hide from your face? If I go up to heaven [eternity], *you're there! If I go down to the realm of the dead, you're there too! If I fly with wings into the shining dawn [tomorrow], you're there! If I fly into the radiant sunset [yesterday], you're there waiting. Wherever I go, your hand will guide me; your strength will empower me.*

—Psalm 139:7-10 TPT

You keep every promise you've ever made to me! Since your love for me is constant and endless, I ask you, Lord, to finish every good thing that you've begun in me!

—Psalm 138:8 TPT

Trust in the Lord with all your heart, and lean not on your own understanding; in all your ways acknowledge Him, and He shall direct your paths.

—Proverbs 3:5-6

Where there is no counsel, the people fall; but in the multitude of counselors there is safety.

—Proverbs 11:14

He has made everything beautiful in its time. Also He has put eternity in their hearts, except that no one can find out the work that God does from beginning to end.

—Ecclesiastes 3:11

My sheep hear My voice, and I know them, and they follow Me.

—John 10:27

I beseech you therefore, brethren, by the mercies of God, that you present your bodies a living sacrifice, holy, acceptable to God, which is your reasonable service. And do not be conformed to this world, but be transformed by the renewing of your mind, that you may prove what is that good and acceptable and perfect will of God.

—Romans 12:1-2

For this is the will of God, your sanctification: that you should abstain from sexual immorality.

—1 Thessalonians 4:3

As each one has received a gift, minister it to one another, as good stewards of the manifold grace of God.

—1 Peter 4:10

Full Disclosure: Asking the Lord to Search Your Heart

O Lord, You have searched me and known me. You know my sitting down and my rising up; You understand my thought afar off. You comprehend my path and my lying down, and are acquainted with all my ways. For there is not a word on my tongue, but behold, O Lord, You know it altogether. You have hedged me behind and before, and laid Your hand upon me.

—Psalm 139:1-5

Search me, O God, and know my heart; try me, and know my anxieties.

—Psalm 139:23

And see if there is any wicked way in me, and lead me in the way everlasting.

—Psalm 139:24

But You, O Lord, know me; You have seen me, and You have tested my heart toward You....

—Jeremiah 12:3

I, the Lord, search the heart, I test the mind, even to give every man according to his ways, according to the fruit of his doings.

—Jeremiah 17:10

But the Lord said to Samuel, "Do not look at his appearance or at his physical stature, because I have refused him. For the Lord does not see as man sees; for man looks at the outward appearance, but the Lord looks at the heart."

—1 Samuel 16:7

He who searches the hearts knows what the mind of the Spirit is, because He makes intercession for the saints according to the will of God.

—Romans 8:27

As for you, my son Solomon, know the God of your father, and serve Him with a loyal heart and with a willing mind; for the Lord searches all hearts and understands all the intent of the thoughts. If you seek Him, He will be found by you; but if you forsake Him, He will cast you off forever.

—1 Chronicles 28:9

I will kill her children with death, and all the churches shall know that I am He who searches the minds and hearts. And I will give to each one of you according to your works.

—Revelation 2:23

Break the arm of the wicked and the evil man; seek out his wickedness until You find none.

—Psalm 10:15

The Lord shall preserve your going out and your coming in from this time forth, and even forevermore.

—Psalm 121:8

You are so intimately aware of me, Lord. You read my heart like an open book and you know all the words I'm about to speak before I even start a sentence! You know every step I will take before my journey even begins. You've gone into the future to prepare the way, and in kindness you follow behind me to spare me from the hurt of my past. With your hand of love upon my life, you impart a blessing to me.

Psalm 139:3-5 TPT

Trust in the Lord with all your heart, and lean not on your own understanding; in all your ways acknowledge Him, and He shall direct your paths.

Proverbs 3:5-6

Power of Prophetic Acts

> *And so it was, when Moses held up his hand, that Israel prevailed; and when he let down his hand, Amalek prevailed. But Moses' hands became heavy; so they took a stone and put it under him, and he sat on it. And Aaron and Hur supported his hands, one on one side, and the other on the other side; and his hands were steady until the going down of the sun. So Joshua defeated Amalek and his people with the edge of the sword.*
>
> —Exodus 17:11-13

> *Then Joshua spoke to the Lord in the day when the Lord delivered up the Amorites before the children of Israel, and he said in the sight of Israel: "Sun, stand still over Gibeon; and Moon, in the Valley of Aijalon." So the sun stood still, and the moon stopped, till the people had revenge upon their enemies. Is this not written in the Book of Jasher? So the sun stood still in the midst of heaven, and did not hasten to go down for about a whole day. And there has been no day like that, before it or after it, that the Lord heeded the voice of a man; for the Lord fought for Israel.*
>
> —Joshua 10:12-14

> *Then Samuel took the horn of oil and anointed him in the midst of his brothers; and the Spirit of the*

Lord came upon David from that day forward. So Samuel arose and went to Ramah.

—1 Samuel 16:13

So Ahab went up to eat and drink. And Elijah went up to the top of Carmel; then he bowed down on the ground, and put his face between his knees, and said to his servant, "Go up now, look toward the sea." So he went up and looked, and said, "There is nothing." And seven times he said, "Go again." Then it came to pass the seventh time, that he said, "There is a cloud, as small as a man's hand, rising out of the sea!" So he said, "Go up, say to Ahab, 'Prepare your chariot, and go down before the rain stops you.'"

—1 Kings 18:42-44

So he departed from there, and found Elisha the son of Shaphat, who was plowing with twelve yoke of oxen before him, and he was with the twelfth. Then Elijah passed by him and threw his mantle on him.

—1 Kings 19:19

Then Naaman went with his horses and chariot, and he stood at the door of Elisha's house. And Elisha sent a messenger to him, saying, "Go and wash in the Jordan seven times, and your flesh shall be restored to you, and you shall be clean." But Naaman became furious, and went away and said, "Indeed," I said to myself, "He will surely come out to me, and stand and call on the name of the Lord his God, and wave his hand over the place, and heal the leprosy. Are not the Abanah and the Pharpar, the rivers of Damascus, better than all the waters of Israel? Could I not wash in them and be clean?" So he turned and went away in a rage. And his servants came near and spoke to him, and said, "My father, if the prophet had told you to do something great, would you not have done it? How much more then, when he says to you, 'Wash, and be clean'?" So he went down and dipped seven times in the Jordan, according to the saying of the man of God; and his flesh was restored like the flesh of a little child, and he was clean.

—2 KINGS 5:9-14

And Elisha said to him, "Take a bow and some arrows." So he took himself a bow and some arrows. Then he said to the king of Israel, "Put your hand on the bow." So he put his hand on it, and Elisha put his hands on the king's hands. And he said, "Open the east window"; and he opened it. Then Elisha said, "Shoot"; and he shot. And he said, "The arrow of the Lord's deliverance and the arrow of deliverance from Syria; for you must strike the Syrians at Aphek till you have destroyed them." Then he said, "Take the arrows"; so he took them. And he said to the king of Israel, "Strike the ground"; so he struck three times, and stopped. And the man of God was angry with him, and said, "You should have struck five or six times; then you would have struck Syria till you had destroyed it! But now you will strike Syria only three times."

—2 KINGS 13:15-19

Then the Lord said, "Just as My servant Isaiah has walked naked and barefoot three years for a sign and a wonder against Egypt and Ethiopia, so shall the king of Assyria lead away the Egyptians as prisoners and the Ethiopians as captives, young and old, naked and barefoot, with their buttocks uncovered, to the shame of Egypt. Then they shall be afraid and ashamed of Ethiopia their expectation and Egypt their glory."

—ISAIAH 20:3-5

When the Lord began to speak by Hosea, the Lord said to Hosea: "Go, take yourself a wife of harlotry and children of harlotry, For the land has committed great harlotry by departing from the Lord."

—HOSEA 1:2

Lie also on your left side, and lay the iniquity of the house of Israel upon it. According to the number of the days that you lie on it, you shall bear their iniquity. For I have laid on you the years of their iniquity, according to the number of the days, three hundred and ninety days; so you shall bear the iniquity of the house of Israel. And when you have completed them, lie again on your right side; then you shall bear the iniquity of the house of Judah forty days. I have laid on you a day for each year.

—Ezekiel 4:4-6

And you, son of man, take a sharp sword, take it as a barber's razor, and pass it over your head and your beard; then take scales to weigh and divide the hair. You shall burn with fire one-third in the midst of the city, when the days of the siege are finished; then you shall take one-third and strike around it with the sword, and one-third you shall scatter in the wind: I will draw out a sword after them. You shall also take a small number of them and bind them in the edge of your garment. Then take some of them again and throw them into the midst of the fire, and burn them in the fire. From there a fire will go out into all the house of Israel.

—Ezekiel 5:1-4

Then the Lord put forth His hand and touched my mouth, and the Lord said to me: "Behold, I have put My words in your mouth. See, I have this day set you over the nations and over the kingdoms, to root out and to pull down, to destroy and to throw down, to build and to plant."

—Jeremiah 1:9-10

And as they were eating, Jesus took bread, blessed and broke it, and gave it to them and said, "Take, eat; this is My body." Then He took the cup, and when He had given thanks He gave it to them, and they all drank from it. And He said to them, "This is My blood of the new covenant, which is shed for many. Assuredly, I say to you, I will no longer drink of the fruit of the vine until that day when I drink it new in the kingdom of God."

—Mark 14:22-25

And they cast out many demons, and anointed with oil many who were sick, and healed them.

—Mark 6:13

Now a woman, having a flow of blood for twelve years, who had spent all her livelihood on physicians and could not be healed by any, came from behind and touched the border of His garment. And immediately her flow of blood stopped. And Jesus said, "Who touched Me?" When all denied it, Peter and those with him said, "Master, the multitudes throng and press You, and You say, 'Who touched Me?'" But Jesus said, "Somebody touched Me, for I perceived power going out from Me."

—Luke 8:43-46

When He had said these things, He spat on the ground and made clay with the saliva; and He anointed the eyes of the blind man with the clay. And He said to him, "Go, wash in the pool of Siloam" (which is translated, Sent). So he went and washed, and came back seeing.

—John 9:6-7

Then Mary took a pound of very costly oil of spikenard, anointed the feet of Jesus, and wiped His feet with her hair. And the house was filled with the fragrance of the oil. ...But Jesus said, "Let her alone. She has kept this for the day of My burial."

—John 12:3,7

And as we stayed many days, a certain prophet named Agabus came down from Judea. When he had come to us, he took Paul's belt, bound his own hands and feet, and said, "Thus says the Holy Spirit, 'So shall the Jews at Jerusalem bind the man who owns this belt, and deliver him into the hands of the Gentiles.'" Now when we heard these things, both we and those from that place pleaded with him not to go up to Jerusalem.

—Acts 21:10-12

Power of Declaring and Decreeing

Then He said, "I will make all My goodness pass before you, and I will proclaim the name of the Lord before you. I will be gracious to whom I will be gracious, and I will have compassion on whom I will have compassion."

—Exodus 33:19

I call heaven and earth as witnesses today against you, that I have set before you life and death, blessing and cursing; therefore choose life, that both you and your descendants may live.

—Deuteronomy 30:19

However, in the first year of Cyrus king of Babylon, King Cyrus issued a decree to build this house of God.

—Ezra 5:13

So the decree of Esther confirmed these matters of Purim, and it was written in the book.

—Esther 9:32

You will also declare a thing, and it will be established for you; so light will shine on your ways.

—Job 22:28

I will declare the decree: The Lord has said to Me, "You are My Son, today I have begotten You."

—Psalm 2:7

He also established them forever and ever; He made a decree which shall not pass away.

—Psalm 148:6

The mouth of the righteous brings forth wisdom, but the perverse tongue will be cut out.

—Proverbs 10:31

A man will be satisfied with good by the fruit of his mouth, and the recompense of a man's hands will be rendered to him.

—Proverbs 12:14

There is one who speaks like the piercings of a sword, but the tongue of the wise promotes health.

—Proverbs 12:18

He who guards his mouth preserves his life, but he who opens wide his lips shall have destruction.

—Proverbs 13:3

A wholesome tongue is a tree of life, but perverseness in it breaks the spirit.

—Proverbs 15:4

Whoever guards his mouth and tongue keeps his soul from troubles.

—Proverbs 21:23

And he caused it to be proclaimed and published throughout Nineveh by the decree of the king and his nobles, saying, "Let neither man nor beast, herd nor flock, taste anything; do not let them eat, or drink water."

—Jonah 3:7

Woe to those who decree unrighteous decrees, who write misfortune, which they have prescribed.

—Isaiah 10:1

Thus says the Lord, the Holy One of Israel, and his Maker: "Ask Me of things to come concerning My sons; and concerning the work of My hands, you command Me."

—Isaiah 45:11

So shall My word be that goes forth from My mouth; it shall not return to Me void, but it shall accomplish what I please, and it shall prosper in the thing for which I sent it.

—Isaiah 55:11

And the man said to me, "Son of man, look with your eyes and hear with your ears, and fix your mind on everything I show you; for you were brought here so that I might show them to you. Declare to the house of Israel everything you see."

—Ezekiel 40:4

For by your words you will be justified, and by your words you will be condemned.

—Matthew 12:37

Not what goes into the mouth defiles a man; but what comes out of the mouth, this defiles a man.

—Matthew 15:11

For assuredly, I say to you, whoever says to this mountain, "Be removed and be cast into the sea," and does not doubt in his heart, but believes that those things he says will be done, he will have whatever he says.

—Mark 11:23

(As it is written, "I have made you a father of many nations") in the presence of Him whom he believed—God, who gives life to the dead and calls those things which do not exist as though they did.

—Romans 4:17

Knowing When God Is Doing Something New in Your Life

Behold, I will do a new thing, now it shall spring forth; shall you not know it? I will even make a road in the wilderness and rivers in the desert.

—Isaiah 43:19

Yet the Lord has not given you a heart to perceive and eyes to see and ears to hear, to this very day.

—Deuteronomy 29:4

Lord, You have heard the desire of the humble; You will prepare their heart; You will cause Your ear to hear.

—Psalm 10:17

My mouth shall speak wisdom, and the meditation of my heart shall give understanding.

—Psalm 49:3

From the end of the earth I will cry to You, when my heart is overwhelmed; lead me to the rock that is higher than I.

—Psalm 61:2

Counsel in the heart of man is like deep water, but a man of understanding will draw it out.

—Proverbs 20:5

And the Lord said to me, "Son of man, mark well, see with your eyes and hear with your ears, all that I say to you concerning all the ordinances of the house of the Lord and all its laws. Mark well who may enter the house and all who go out from the sanctuary."

—Ezekiel 44:5

He who has ears to hear, let him hear!

—Matthew 11:15

He who has ears to hear, let him hear!

—Matthew 13:9

But blessed are your eyes for they see, and your ears for they hear.

—Matthew 13:16

Then the righteous will shine forth as the sun in the kingdom of their Father. He who has ears to hear, let him hear!

—Matthew 13:43

If anyone has ears to hear, let him hear.

—Mark 4:23

If anyone has ears to hear, let him hear!

—Mark 7:16

Therefore I speak to them in parables, because seeing they do not see, and hearing they do not hear, nor do they understand. And in them the prophecy of Isaiah is fulfilled, which says: "Hearing you will hear and shall not understand, and seeing you will see and not perceive; for the hearts of this people have grown dull. Their ears are hard of hearing, and their eyes they have closed, lest they should see with their eyes and hear with their ears, lest they should understand with their hearts and turn, so that I should heal them." But blessed are your eyes for they see, and your ears for they hear; for assuredly, I say to you that many prophets and righteous men desired to see what you see, and did not see it, and to hear what you hear, and did not hear it.

—MATTHEW 13:13-17

He who has an ear, let him hear what the Spirit says to the churches. To him who overcomes I will give to eat from the tree of life, which is in the midst of the Paradise of God.

—REVELATION 2:7

Marking and Noting When God Is Doing Something New and Amazing

Oh, that I had one to hear me! Here is my mark. Oh, that the Almighty would answer me, that my Prosecutor had written a book!

—JOB 31:35

Do you know the time when the wild mountain goats bear young? Or can you mark when the deer gives birth?

—JOB 39:1

For who has stood in the counsel of the Lord, and has perceived and heard His word? Who has marked His word and heard it?

JEREMIAH 23:18

Let not mercy and truth forsake you; bind them around your neck, write them on the tablet of your heart.

—Proverbs 3:3

I acknowledged my sin to You, and my iniquity I have not hidden. I said, "I will confess my transgressions to the Lord," and You forgave the iniquity of my sin. Selah.

—Psalm 32:5

For I acknowledge my transgressions, and my sin is always before me.

—Psalm 51:3

So God, who knows the heart, acknowledged them by giving them the Holy Spirit, just as He did to us.

—Acts 15:8

The Responsibility and Power of Celebrating What God Is Doing

It shall be to you a sabbath of solemn rest, and you shall afflict your souls; on the ninth day of the month at evening, from evening to evening, you shall celebrate your sabbath.

—Leviticus 23:32

He is your praise, and He is your God, who has done for you these great and awesome things which your eyes have seen.

—Deuteronomy 10:21

Then David danced before the Lord with all his might; and David was wearing a linen ephod.

—2 Samuel 6:14

So they brought the ark of the Lord, and set it in its place in the midst of the tabernacle that David had erected for it. Then David offered burnt offerings and peace offerings before the Lord.

—2 Samuel 6:17

Then the children of Israel, the priests and the Levites and the rest of the descendants of the captivity, celebrated the dedication of this house of God with joy.

—Ezra 6:16

Now at the dedication of the wall of Jerusalem they sought out the Levites in all their places, to bring them to Jerusalem to celebrate the dedication with gladness, both with thanksgivings and singing, with cymbals and stringed instruments and harps.

—Nehemiah 12:27

Therefore the Jews of the villages who dwelt in the unwalled towns celebrated the fourteenth day of the month of Adar with gladness and feasting, as a holiday, and for sending presents to one another.

—Esther 9:19

As the days on which the Jews had rest from their enemies, as the month which was turned from sorrow to joy for them, and from mourning to a holiday; that they should make them days of feasting and joy, of sending presents to one another and gifts to the poor.

—Esther 9:22

The Jews established and imposed it upon themselves and their descendants and all who would join them, that without fail they should celebrate these two days every year, according to the written instructions and according to the prescribed time.

—Esther 9:27

Oh, clap your hands, all you peoples! Shout to God with the voice of triumph!

—Psalm 47:1

Let my mouth be filled with Your praise and with Your glory all the day.

—Psalm 71:8

Men shall speak of the might of Your awesome acts, and I will declare Your greatness. They shall utter the memory of Your great goodness, and shall sing of Your righteousness. The Lord is gracious and full of compassion, slow to anger and great in mercy.

—Psalm 145:6-8

Praise the Lord! For it is good to sing praises to our God; for it is pleasant, and praise is beautiful.

—Psalm 147:1

I know that nothing is better for them than to rejoice, and to do good in their lives, and also that every man should eat and drink and enjoy the good of all his labor—it is the gift of God.

—Ecclesiastes 3:12-13

So I perceived that nothing is better than that a man should rejoice in his own works, for that is his heritage....

—Ecclesiastes 3:22

Then the multitudes who went before and those who followed cried out, saying: "Hosanna to the Son of David! 'Blessed is He who comes in the name of the Lord!' Hosanna in the highest!"

—Matthew 21:9

In this you greatly rejoice, though now for a little while, if need be, you have been grieved by various trials, that the genuineness of your faith, being much more precious than gold that perishes, though it is tested by fire, may be found to praise, honor, and glory at the revelation of Jesus Christ, whom having not seen you love. Though now you do not see Him, yet believing, you rejoice with joy inexpressible and full of glory, receiving the end of your faith—the salvation of your souls.

—1 Peter 1:6-9

Newness of Life and Being a New Creation

Therefore, if anyone is in Christ, he is a new creation; old things have passed away; behold, all things have become new.

—2 Corinthians 5:17

For in Christ Jesus neither circumcision nor uncircumcision avails anything, but a new creation.

—Galatians 6:15

For behold, I create new heavens and a new earth; and the former shall not be remembered or come to mind.

—Isaiah 65:17

Then He who sat on the throne said, "Behold, I make all things new." And He said to me, "Write, for these words are true and faithful."

—Revelation 21:5

Therefore we were buried with Him through baptism into death, that just as Christ was raised from the dead by the glory of the Father, even so we also should walk in newness of life.

—Romans 6:4

But now we have been delivered from the law, having died to what we were held by, so that we should serve in the newness of the Spirit and not in the oldness of the letter.

—Romans 7:6

The Practice and Exercise of Spiritual Gifts and the Prophetic

Then the anointed priest shall take some of the bull's blood and bring it to the tabernacle of meeting.

—Leviticus 4:5

Now Joshua the son of Nun was full of the spirit of wisdom, for Moses had laid his hands on him; so the children of Israel heeded him, and did as the Lord had commanded Moses.

—Deuteronomy 34:9

And it shall come to pass afterward that I will pour out My Spirit on all flesh; your sons and your daughters shall prophesy, your old men shall dream dreams, your young men shall see visions.

—Joel 2:28

Again He said to me, "Prophesy to these bones, and say to them, 'O dry bones, hear the word of the Lord! Thus says the Lord God to these bones: "Surely I will cause breath to enter into you, and you shall live. I will put sinews on you and bring flesh upon you, cover you with skin and put breath in you; and you shall live. Then you shall know that I am the Lord."'" So I prophesied as I was commanded; and as I prophesied, there was a noise, and suddenly a rattling; and the bones came together, bone to bone. Indeed, as I looked, the sinews and the flesh came upon them, and the skin covered them over; but there was no breath in them.

—Ezekiel 37:4-8

And He took them up in His arms, laid His hands on them, and blessed them.

—Mark 10:16

They will take up serpents; and if they drink anything deadly, it will by no means hurt them; they will lay hands on the sick, and they will recover.

—Mark 16:18

When the sun was setting, all those who had any that were sick with various diseases brought them to Him; and He laid His hands on every one of them and healed them.

—Luke 4:40

And they were all filled with the Holy Spirit and began to speak with other tongues, as the Spirit gave them utterance. And there were dwelling in Jerusalem Jews, devout men, from every nation under heaven. And when this sound occurred, the multitude came together, and were confused, because everyone heard them speak in his own language. Then they were all amazed and marveled, saying to one another, "Look, are not all these who speak Galileans? And how is it that we hear, each in our own language in which we were born? Parthians and Medes and Elamites, those dwelling in Mesopotamia, Judea and Cappadocia, Pontus and Asia, Phrygia and Pamphylia, Egypt and the parts of Libya adjoining Cyrene, visitors from Rome, both Jews and proselytes, Cretans and Arabs—we hear them speaking in our own tongues the wonderful works of God." So they were all amazed and perplexed, saying to one another, "Whatever could this mean?"

—Acts 2:4-12

Then they laid hands on them, and they received the Holy Spirit.

—Acts 8:17

And the saying pleased the whole multitude. And they chose Stephen, a man full of faith and the Holy Spirit, and Philip, Prochorus, Nicanor, Timon, Parmenas, and Nicolas, a proselyte from Antioch, whom they set before the apostles; and when they had prayed, they laid hands on them.

—Acts 6:5-6

And when Paul had laid hands on them, the Holy Spirit came upon them, and they spoke with tongues and prophesied.

—Acts 19:6

And though I have the gift of prophecy, and understand all mysteries and all knowledge, and though I have all faith, so that I could remove mountains, but have not love, I am nothing.

—1 Corinthians 13:2

Pursue love, and desire spiritual gifts, but especially that you may prophesy. For he who speaks in a tongue does not speak to men but to God, for no one understands him; however, in the spirit he speaks mysteries. But he who prophesies speaks edification and exhortation and comfort to men. He who speaks in a tongue edifies himself, but he who prophesies edifies the church.

—1 Corinthians 14:1-4

When they heard this, they were baptized in the name of the Lord Jesus. And when Paul had laid hands on them, the Holy Spirit came upon them, and they spoke with tongues and prophesied.

—Acts 19:5-6

And it happened that the father of Publius lay sick of a fever and dysentery. Paul went in to him and prayed, and he laid his hands on him and healed him.

—Acts 28:8

Do not neglect the gift that is in you, which was given to you by prophecy with the laying on of the hands of the eldership.

—1 Timothy 4:14

Therefore I remind you to stir up the gift of God which is in you through the laying on of my hands.

—2 Timothy 1:6

For prophecy never came by the will of man, but holy men of God spoke as they were moved by the Holy Spirit.

—2 Peter 1:21

About Troy Brewer

Troy Brewer is a tireless student of God's Word and sold-out believer in all things prophetic. Pastor at OpenDoor Church in Burleson, Texas, Troy's radio and television programs are broadcast worldwide. He is a global missionary known for his radical love for Jesus, unique teaching style, and his passion for serving people. Troy rescues girls and boys from sex trafficking worldwide through his ministry, Troy Brewer Ministries.

OTHER BOOKS BY TROY A. BREWER

Numbers That Preach

Living Life /Forward

Good Overcomes Evil

Looking Up

Soul Invasion

Daily Transformation Devotional

Miracles with a Message

Best of the Brewer